Jacob

Jacob meets Leah and Rachel, the daughters of Laban, who will become his wives and the mothers of his many children.

Money at its Best: Millionaires of the Bible

Abraham and Sarah
Daniel
David
Esther
Jacob
Job

Joseph
Moses
Noah
Samson
Solomon
Wealth in Biblical Times

Jacob

Benjamin T. Hoak

Mason Crest Publishers
Philadelphia

Produced by OTTN Publishing, Stockton, NJ.
Cover design © 2008 TLC Graphics, www.TLCGraphics.com.

Mason Crest Publishers
370 Reed Road, Suite 302
Broomall PA 19008
www.masoncrest.com

Copyright © 2009 by Mason Crest Publishers. All rights reserved.
Printed and bound in the United States of America.

First printing

1 3 5 7 9 8 6 4 2

Library of Congress Cataloging-in-Publication Data

Hoak, Benjamin T.
  Jacob / by Benjamin T. Hoak.
     p. cm. — (Money at its best : millionaires of the Old Testament)
  Includes bibliographical references.
  ISBN 978-1-4222-0470-2
  ISBN 978-1-4222-0845-8 (pbk.)
  1. Jacob (Biblical patriarch)—Juvenile literature. 2. Bible. O.T.—Biography—Juvenile literature. I. Title.
  BS580.J3H63 2008
  222'.11092—dc22
                                    2008020866

Publisher's Note: The Web sites listed in this book were active at the time of publication. The publisher is not responsible for Web sites that have changed their address or discontinued operation since the date of publication. The publisher reviews and updates the Web sites each time the book is reprinted.

Table of Contents

Jacob and His Wealth	6
Introduction: Wealth and Faith	7
1. Why Jacob?	11
2. Early Years	15
3. Deception	24
4. Dreams and Marriage	34
5. Building a Family and a Fortune	46
6. Return to Canaan	57
7. Wrestling and Reconciliation	69
8. Rachel's Death and Joseph's Life	81
9. Joseph in Egypt	93
10. A New Home	104
11. Final Resting Place	115
Notes	126
Glossary	132
Further Reading	135
Internet Resources	136
Index	138
Illustration Credits	143
About the Author	144

Jacob and His Wealth

- Although Jacob was Isaac's younger son, he received the blessing and the birthright due to the eldest. This meant he received the largest share of his father's estate. Isaac himself was very rich by the standards of biblical times, when wealth was measured by huge flocks of livestock, extensive landholdings, large families, and unlimited staffs of servants.

- After spending two decades working for his father-in-law, a man named Laban, Jacob describes how he always endeavored to do his best: "I have been with you for twenty years now. Your sheep and goats have not miscarried, nor have I eaten rams from your flocks. I did not bring you animals torn by wild beasts; I bore the loss myself. And you demanded payment from me for whatever was stolen by day or night. This was my situation: The heat consumed me in the daytime and the cold at night, and sleep fled from my eyes. . . . [Y]ou changed my wages ten times. If the God of my father, the God of Abraham and the Fear of Isaac, had not been with me, you would surely have sent me away empty-handed. (Genesis 31:38-40, 41-42). However, despite Laban's injustices, God helps Jacob create his own wealth. "[Jacob] grew exceedingly prosperous and came to own large flocks, and maidservants and menservants, and camels and donkeys. (Genesis 30:43).

- Jacob's possessions are so great that when he returns to Canaan, he is able to give his estranged brother Esau a rich present—220 goats, 220 sheep, 30 female camels, 50 head of cattle, and 30 donkeys (Genesis 32:13-15).

- God promises to fulfill his covenant with Abraham through Jacob and his descendants: "And God said to him, "I am God Almighty; be fruitful and increase in number. A nation and a community of nations will come from you, and kings will come from your body. The land I gave to Abraham and Isaac I also give to you, and I will give this land to your descendants after you" (Genesis 35:11-13).

- Although Jacob works hard and is blessed by God, he is also cunning and manipulative, particular in his younger years. He cheats his brother Esau; in turn, Jacob is cheated by Laban. Throughout his life he succumbs to negativity and depression, forgetting that God is in control. At times he trusts God; at other times, he sinks into despair. Thus Jacob is never able to fully enjoy the many blessings that God has given to him. Near the end of his life, he tells Egypt's Pharaoh, "My years have been few and difficult" (Genesis 47:9).

Introduction: Wealth and Faith

Many people believe strongly that great personal wealth is incompatible with deep religious belief—that like oil and water, the two cannot be mixed. Christians, in particular, often feel this way, recollecting Jesus Christ's own teachings on wealth. "Do not store up for yourselves treasures on earth, where moth and rust destroy, and where thieves break in and steal," Jesus cautions during the Sermon on the Mount (Matthew 6:19). In Luke 18:25, he declares, "It is easier for a camel to go through the eye of a needle than for a rich man to enter the kingdom of God"—a sentiment repeated elsewhere in the Gospels.

Yet in Judeo-Christian culture there is a long-standing tradition of material wealth as the manifestation of God's blessing. This tradition is amply reflected in the books of the Hebrew Bible (or as Christians know them, the Old Testament). Genesis 13:2 says that the patriarch Abram (Abraham) "had become very wealthy in livestock and in silver and gold"; the Bible makes it clear that this prosperity is a gift from God. Other figures whose lives are chronicled in

Genesis—including Isaac, Jacob, Joseph, Noah, and Job—are described as both wealthy and righteous. The book of Deuteronomy expresses God's promise of prosperity for those who obey his commandments:

> If you fully obey the Lord your God and carefully follow all his commands I give you today, the Lord your God will set you high above all the nations on earth. . . . The Lord will grant you abundant prosperity—in the fruit of your womb, the young of your livestock and the crops of your ground—in the land he swore to your forefathers to give you. (Deuteronomy 28:1, 11)

A key requirement for this prosperity, however, is that God's blessings must be used to help others. Deuteronomy 15:10–11 says, "Give generously . . . and do so without a grudging heart; then because of this the Lord your God will bless you in all your work and in everything you put your hand to." The book of Proverbs—written during the time of Solomon, one of history's wealthiest rulers—similarly presents wealth as a desirable blessing that can be obtained through hard work, wisdom, and following God's laws. Proverbs 14:31 promises, "The faithless will be fully repaid for their ways, and the good man rewarded for his."

Numerous stories and folktales show the generosity of the patriarchs. According to Jewish legend, Job owned an inn at a crossroads, where he allowed travelers to eat and drink at no cost. When they offered to pay, he instead told them about God, explaining that he was simply a steward of the wealth that God had given to him and urging them to worship God, obey God's commands, and receive their own blessings. A story about Abraham says that when he moved his flocks from one field to another, he would muzzle the animals so that they would not graze on a neighbor's property.

After the death of Solomon, however, the kingdom of Israel

was divided and the people fell away from the commandments God had mandated. The later writings of the prophets, who are attempting to correct misbehavior, specifically address unethical acts committed to gain wealth. "You trample on the poor," complained the prophet Amos. "You oppress the righteous and take bribes and you deprive the poor of justice in the courts" (Amos 5:11, 12). The prophet Isaiah insists, "Learn to do right! Seek justice, encourage the oppressed. . . . If you are willing and obedient, you will eat the best from the land; but if you resist and rebel, you will be devoured by the sword" (Isaiah 1:17, 19–20).

Viewed in this light, the teachings of Jesus take on new meaning. Jesus does not condemn wealth; he condemns those who would allow the pursuit of wealth to come ahead of the proper relationship with God: "No one can serve two masters. . . . You cannot serve both God and money" (Matthew 6:24).

Today, nearly everyone living in the Western world could be considered materially wealthier than the people of the Bible, who had no running water or electricity, lived in tents, walked when traveling long distances, and wore clothing handmade from animal skins. But we also live in an age when tabloid newspapers and trashy television programs avidly follow the misadventures of spoiled and selfish millionaire athletes and entertainers. In the mainstream news outlets, it is common to read or hear reports of corporate greed and malfeasance, or of corrupt politicians enriching themselves at the expense of their constituents. Often, the responsibility of the wealthy to those members of the community who are not as successful seems to have been forgotten.

The purpose of the series MONEY AT ITS BEST: MILLIONAIRES OF THE BIBLE is to examine the lives of key figures from biblical history, showing how these people used their wealth or their powerful and privileged positions in order to make a difference in the lives of others.

Jacob and the ladder of his dream, which reaches from earth to heaven, as described in Genesis 28:11–19. Window from the cathedral at Freiburg im Breisgau, Germany.

WHY JACOB?

The Jewish religion begins with three patriarchs: Abraham, Isaac, and Jacob. God sets in motion his redemptive relationship with the nation of Israel by establishing a covenant with Abraham, who until that time has been a simple shepherd in the land of Ur. In the covenant, God promises him descendants who cannot be numbered, as well as a space for them to occupy—the land of Canaan. As Abraham ages, the covenant relationship passes to Isaac, the miracle son of his old age. Isaac continues to abide by the covenant, and he has two children, Esau and Jacob, twin brothers who are destined both for trouble and for great things.

God chooses to continue his covenant through Jacob, the younger (by mere minutes) of the twins and the last of the traditional patriarchs. Jacob grows up quiet and reserved, a tent dweller who cares more about scholarship than hunting, although he does learn the basics of shepherding. He swindles his brother Esau out of his birthright and then later, at the urging of his mother, deceives his father in order to obtain the firstborn blessing that should have also gone to Esau.

Fearing for his life, Jacob flees to the far-off house of his mother's relatives, where he marries two women and produces 12 sons (the tribes of Israel are later named for these sons and 2 grandsons). While there, he builds a fortune in flocks, herds, and servants, despite attempts by his father-in-law to cheat him out of his earnings. After more than 20 years away, he returns to Canaan, where he lives until 11 of his sons sell Joseph, his favorite son, into Egyptian slavery. This spins Jacob into a spiral of depression, misery, and passivity that he only snaps out of when he learns Joseph is still alive and is summoning him to Egypt, where Joseph is now second in command of the entire nation. Jacob lives the last 17 years of his life in contentment in Egypt, watching as his descendants continue to multiply before his eyes.

Jacob knows God and speaks intimately with him. He is smart and persistent, and he builds a fortune in flocks, herds, and servants. He fathers a nation. And yet for all that, for all his privileges and wealth and lineage, Jacob's behavior seems to suggest he is trying to throw it all away. He has another side that is not as squeaky clean—in fact, it is downright dirty. His struggles start early—Jacob's life "was marked by conflict and strife from before day one," says one scholar. "Even in the womb, life was a struggle for Jacob." His conflicts expand to include his parents, wives, children, father-in-law, and God.

Jacob is cunning and manipulative, maneuvering his way to where he thinks he needs to be, depending too much upon his own schemes rather than God's promises.

He is impulsive and foolish, often choosing half-hearted obedience rather than whole-souled devotion to God. He marries two wives, which leads to a host of problems. In his later years he is passive when he should be active, and he lets his boys rule the roost. He succumbs to negativity and depression, forgetting that God is still in control. At times he trusts God; at other times, he sinks into despair. At the end of their lives, Abraham and Isaac both reflect on how full and good their days have been. Jacob, on the other hand, wearily remarks how bitter his life has been.

One of the main family traits that Jacob displays—and passes on—is trickery, or deception. He cheats his brother out of his birthright. His mother helps him deceive his father in order to obtain Esau's blessing. His uncle tricks him into marrying the wrong daughter. His wives manipulate him to gain more children. His sons deceive the men of a city in order to kill them all. These are not typical characteristics of an exemplary family, let alone one that is supposed to lead a nation. Imperfection is rampant.

Jacob (center), encouraged by his mother Rebekah, deceives his nearly blind father Isaac in order to receive the blessing normally given to the firstborn son.

But imperfect people are the ones God chooses to build his nation. And over the course of his life, Jacob begins to live up to the expectations God has for him until he embraces his role and trusts God to deliver on his promises.

Jacob plays a major role in Judaism and Christianity as one of the patriarchs of Israel; indeed, God later renames him Israel, from which the nation takes its name. He is a lesser figure in Islam, but he is mentioned 16 times in the Qur'an, mostly in connection with Joseph (an entire sura, or chapter, is given over to Joseph) or in company with Abraham and Isaac. The Qur'an calls him a prophet to whom God reveals his will and upon whom God bestows gifts and renown. It also speaks of him as a righteous man who serves God, and a man of might and vision who will dwell with God among the righteous.

Because of the host of tensions and struggles in his life, Jacob's story is one of the more interesting in the Bible. There is drama because the reader knows that God wants his covenant to flow through Jacob, but there are real doubts about whether Jacob can handle God's designs. As the *Anchor Bible Dictionary* notes, "It is a central tension . . . whether Jacob will actually become the chosen leader which later Israelites knew him to be."

In the end, he does become that leader, but only because of a transformative process that overcomes many obstacles. Jacob's story, says one scholar, "is virtually unique in ancient literature in its searching representation of the radical transformations a person undergoes in the slow course of time." Especially in the first part of his life, he is "scheming, conniving and calculating," but in the end, "he shows us the triumph of grace over all obstacles." If Abraham is the classic picture of faith, then his grandson Jacob is "the archetypal picture of grace."

Early Years

To put the story of Jacob in context, the modern reader must start with his great-grandfather, Abraham. The entire Jewish nation descends from him, the one with whom God initiates a covenant that lasts for generations. God explains it this way to Abraham:

> "Behold, my covenant is with you, and you shall be the father of a multitude of nations. . . . I will make you exceedingly fruitful, and I will make you into nations, and kings shall come from you. And I will establish my covenant between me and you and your offspring after you throughout their generations for an everlasting covenant, to be God to you and to your offspring after you. And I will give to you and to your offspring after you the land of your sojournings, all the land of Canaan, for an everlasting possession, and I will be their God." (Crossway Bibles: English Standard Version, 2001; Genesis 17:3–8)

Abraham is 99 years old and childless when God makes the promise, and his wife Sarah is 90. So it requires great faith on his part to believe that God is actually going to create a nation from the descendants he has yet to produce. To keep the covenant, God grants Abraham a son named Isaac; he comes long after the time Abraham and Sarah believe they can bear children. The family settles in Canaan, the land God promised as an inheritance (Canaan covered roughly the area of the current country of Israel). Abraham originally came from Ur, a prosperous city in Mesopotamia far to the east of Canaan, but he also spent quite a bit of time with relatives in Haran, a crossroads trading post in Syria, northeast of Canaan, before he actually took up residence in Canaan. Because of his relatives in Haran, Jacob (Abraham's grandson) later travels there in search of a wife. Jacob ends up spending nearly 20 years of his adult life there, away from Canaan.

Abraham dies at the age of 175, and his sons Isaac and Ishmael bury him in the family tomb that Abraham pur-

Abraham (left), Sarah (seated) and their infant son Isaac, who would become the father of Jacob and Esau. Behind them in this 19th century book illustration are Sarah's slave, Hagar, and Ishmael, Hagar's son by Abraham. The Jewish people are said to be descended from Abraham through Isaac, while the Arabs are descended from Ishmael.

chased—the Cave of Machpelah near Hebron in the land of Canaan.

Jacob's Birth

When he is 40 years old, Isaac marries Rebekah, a relative of Abraham's from the land of Paddan-aram (near Haran). They settle in Beer-lahai-roi, a town located on Canaan's southern border with Egypt. The first thing Genesis records about their relationship after they are married is that "Isaac prayed to the Lord for his wife, because she was barren" (Genesis 25:21). Isaac knew of God's promise to make a great nation of Abraham, which would necessarily include children for him as Abraham and Sarah's sole heir. Isaac and Rebekah's faith is sorely tempted through this trial. God does not answer their prayers and give them children until 20 years into their marriage, when Isaac is 60 years old.

After Rebekah conceives, it soon becomes evident that she is carrying not just one baby, but two. And the pregnancy is not easy—in fact, it is painful, as she often feels the babies struggle within her. She takes this question to God—is she really pregnant? And if so, why does it hurt so much? The answer comes back with consequences bigger

> Ishmael is also Abraham's son, but he was born through Sarah's maid Hagar. Abraham and Sarah were worried she would not conceive, so Sarah gave Hagar to Abraham in an attempt to circumvent God's promise. In the end, Sarah became pregnant with Isaac (the one through whom God continued his covenant), but Ishmael too became the father of millions—tradition has it that he is the father of the Arab race.

than she could have imagined: "'Two nations are in your womb, and two peoples from within you shall be divided; the one shall be stronger than the other, the older shall serve the younger'" (Genesis 25:23).

The two boys, of course, are Jacob and Esau, and they do indeed become the fathers of nations—Esau of Edom and Jacob of Israel. Throughout much of their lives, the two are in conflict with one another. Esau is regarded as the wicked brother, while Jacob is thought of as the righteous one, since God chooses him to continue his covenant. Jewish legend has it that when a pregnant Rebekah would pass a synagogue or Jewish house of worship, Jacob would assert himself by trying to break out of the womb. When Rebekah would walk near a temple erected to idols, Esau would recognize it and begin moving. Either way, the legend says, Rebekah "suffered torturous pain, because her twin sons began their lifelong quarrels in her womb." According to this story, the boys' characters are developed even before they are born.

The Talmud and Midrash

Jewish legends are tales told over centuries that are not included in the Bible, but are often derived from scripture as explanations and expansions of the Talmud and the Midrash. (The Talmud is a compilation of discussions dealing with Jewish law, ethics, custom and history, while the Midrash is a group of Jewish commentaries on the Hebrew scriptures based on exegesis, parables and legends. Rabbis often used the Midrash to fill in gaps in their scriptures.). These collective stories are also called "Haggadah," the Hebrew word for legends of the Bible.

One of the most surprising parts of God's prophesy to Rebekah is that the older son is destined to serve the younger. In the patriarchal society of the time, it was unheard of for a younger brother (even a twin just a few minutes younger) to leapfrog his older brother for precedence in the family. The firstborn son usually received a double share of the inheritance and became the next head of the family. His birthright could be annulled if he committed a terrible act, or it could be sacrificed or transferred legally, as later happened with Jacob and Esau.

As happens with all babies, the twins' time comes to be born. When it does, "The first came out red, all his body like a hairy cloak, so they called his name Esau. Afterward his brother came out with his hand holding Esau's heel, so his name was called Jacob" (Genesis 25:25–26). Esau means "hairy," and his red skin is part of the reason the country named after him was called "Edom," meaning "red." Jacob comes out with his hand on Esau's heel, so his name means "heel catcher" or "supplanter," one who would take the place of his brother. In Hebrew (the language of the Jewish people), Jacob's name is Ya'kov, which is related linguistically to *akev*, the word for heel. The boys' names are especially fitting, given the events of their lives that have yet to unfold.

THE BIRTHRIGHT

The Bible does not give much detail about the twins' childhood, saying only that Esau grows up to be a skillful hunter who loves the outdoors, while Jacob is a quiet man who prefers dwelling in tents, cooking, and working with the flocks and herds. Genesis 25:28 offers a glimpse of a family dynamic that will later cause major problems: "Isaac loved Esau because he ate of his game, but Rebekah loved Jacob." The favoritism of their parents shapes the boys' characters and leads to conflict within

> In Jacob's time, exchangeable money had not yet fully developed, so animals—herds of sheep, goats, and cattle—were just as valuable to their owners as their equivalent value in silver or gold would have been. Thus a person's wealth was typically determined by the size of his herds of livestock.

the family. Jacob later struggles with the same issue in his own family, which contributes to his sons selling their brother Joseph into slavery.

According to Jewish legend, Jacob and Esau both attend school until they come of age at 13. Jacob continues studying after that, but the legend says Esau "abandoned himself to idolatry and an immoral life." Even though he commits evil deeds, the legend says, Esau is able to fool his father with hypocritical conduct, asking him, for example, what tithe God required on straw and salt. He knows those two items are exempt from tithing, so his only goal is to appear pious to his father. Legend also has it that Rebekah is more clear-sighted and so has a greater love for Jacob. Abraham agrees with her because he knows his name will descend through Jacob's line, not Esau's. The legend goes on that the connection between grandfather and grandson is so strong that at the end of Abraham's life, Jacob takes his last meal to him and then lies beside him on the bed as Abraham dies.

Some ancient scholars believe there is more to Jacob than meets the eye—he is not just a simple man abiding at home, but a scholar who works hard at learning. A Jewish Targum of Genesis says that "Jacob was a man perfect in good work, dwelling in schoolhouses," and the ancient book of Jubilees says he learns to write, but Esau does not.

One scholar describes the differences in the twins this way:

> Lordly, selfish, and stirring, yet not without warmth of heart, Esau could not brook the irksome labor of the farm. Let Jacob look after that; the excitement and pleasures of the chase were what he delighted in, and the richer and more luxurious food that a cunning hunter could procure seemed more appropriate to his fastidious palate. Jacob was the very opposite. He was in his element among the flocks and herds, could give his heart to the work of the place, had no recoil from irksome labor, and was pleased with the quiet life of the tent and with plain dishes of herbs.

The Bible's next recorded incident in the brothers' lives introduces the fulfillment of God's prophecy that the older would serve the younger. One day when Jacob is at home

Esau pledges his birthright to Jacob in exchange for a bowl of lentil stew.

preparing lentil stew, Esau arrives exhausted from a hunting expedition. When he sees that Jacob is cooking, he says, "'Let me eat some of that red stew, for I am exhausted!'" (Genesis 25:30). He has likely smelled the food even before he comes inside—cooking lentils produce an aroma that would have been quite attractive to a famished hunter at the end of a long day. (The redness of the stew is part of the play on words that explains why Esau and the nation that descended from him are called "Edom," or "red" in Hebrew.) Jacob, seeing an opportunity, asks for Esau's birthright in exchange for the food. Genesis 25:32–34 records his answer:

> Esau said, "I am about to die; of what use is a birthright to me?" Jacob said, "Swear to me now." So he swore to him and sold his birthright to Jacob. Then Jacob gave Esau bread and lentil stew, and he ate and drank and rose and went his way. Thus Esau despised his birthright.

The exchange leaves an unfavorable impression of both brothers and their relationship. Most siblings would naturally offer food to a starving and exhausted brother, but in this case Esau has to ask for the food, and Jacob will only consider selling it rather than giving it up freely. Jacob drives a hard bargain in obtaining the birthright, and he does it in a scheming, manipulative manner that seems out of place for God's chosen conduit of blessing. As Rabbi Joseph Telushkin says, "Jacob proves quite wily. Aware that people in desperate straits are capable of making extravagant promises they later disavow, he offers Esau the food, but only on condition that he first swear to give up his birthright."

Jacob sees the true value of the birthright—embedded in it is God's promise of blessing and abundance to the

Esau's Major Sins

Jewish legend has it that despising his birthright is only one of five major sins that Esau commits that same day. The others include rape, murder, doubting the resurrection of the dead, and denying God. According to the legend, he is willing to trade away the birthright and its attendant blessing because "the scorn [he] manifested for the resurrection of the dead he felt also for the promise of God to give the Holy Land to the seed of Abraham. He did not believe in it."

seed of Abraham—while Esau despises a lasting privilege to satisfy a temporary condition. He gives up God's blessing, the double portion of his inheritance, and the head of family position that would have one day been his, all for a mess of stew. The Bible elsewhere condemns him for rejecting his rightful inheritance. Hebrews 12:15–16 says, "See to it . . . that no one is . . . unholy (godless) like Esau, who sold his birthright for a single meal." Another scholar says Esau "did not sell it out of hunger, therefore, but because he indeed considered it to be worthless and sold it for nothing."

Jacob now has the birthright, but he cannot yet claim his father's traditional blessing that will pass the line of God's covenant to him. With his mother's help, though, he will soon obtain that blessing through means even more devious than he used to acquire the birthright.

DECEPTION

After Esau sells Jacob his birthright, the family moves to various locations in Canaan as a result of famine, jealous neighbors, and God's direction. God asks them to stay in the land as he expressly renews the covenant he had begun with Abraham:

> And the Lord appeared to him [Isaac] and said, "Do not go down to Egypt; dwell in the land of which I shall tell you. Sojourn in this land, and I will be with you and will bless you, for to you and to your offspring I will give all these lands, and I will establish the oath that I swore to Abraham your father. I will multiply your offspring as the stars of heaven and will give to your offspring all these lands. And in your offspring all the nations of the earth shall be blessed." (Genesis 26:2–4)

Isaac's wealth is also growing as a result of God's covenant blessing upon him.

Genesis 26:12–14 recounts the details: "And Isaac sowed in that land and reaped in the same year a hundredfold. The Lord blessed him, and the man became rich, and gained more and more until he became very wealthy. He had possessions of flocks and herds and many servants, so that the Philistines envied him." Flocks, herds, and servants were more of a measure of wealth than money was in those times, and Isaac is doing so well that the envious residents of the region where he lived ask him to leave their territory because he is now mightier than they are. The hundredfold increase in crop production is also remarkable for the wilderness territory where Isaac resides and is further evidence of God's blessing on him. All this wealth would one day be passed to his sons—and Jacob now has the birthright that entitles him to a double share.

JACOB'S DECEPTION OF ISAAC

The next recorded episode in Jacob's life is "morally problematic," Rabbi Telushkin says, for a man chosen by God to fulfill his covenant. Jacob deceives his father in order to gain the blessing that would rightfully have gone to his older brother. Isaac has become an old man by now, and his eyes are so dim he cannot see. He thinks he is near the end of his life, and he wants to confer his fatherly blessing upon his firstborn son, who will carry on his name and possessions. He calls for Esau and asks him to go out into the fields to hunt game and then prepare the delicious food that he loves so much. After he eats Esau's meal, he plans to bestow the blessing upon him. Rebekah, however, hears his words to Esau and sets her own scheme in motion to gain the blessing for Jacob.

A couple of things are interesting here. First, Isaac either does not know about God's prophecy to Rebekah that their older son will serve their younger son, or he is deliberately ignoring it in order to pass on the traditional rights and privileges to his firstborn son. Second, Isaac and Rebekah apparently are not in the habit of communicating well. This is probably another indicator of the mindset that has led to the favoritism they each show for a particular son. Isaac does not tell Rebekah of his plans to bless Esau—she is left to learn of them through back channels, rather than through a gathering of the family and servants to witness what was supposed to be a momentous event.

Rebekah is so desperate to take by human trickery what God has already promised by divine right that she tells Jacob what she has overheard and commands him to bring two young goats from their flock so she can prepare the delicious food Isaac loves. (The taste of goat would be similar to that of venison. After Rebekah treats the meat with the spices that were common in those times, Isaac will probably not be able to tell that he's eating goat meat rather than the wild venison he had asked for.) Her plan then calls for Jacob to carry the food to his father and impersonate his twin brother in order to gain the blessing. This is just one blatant example of the lying and scheming that Jacob grew up with. Deception seems to recur continually in his family, and the life of his parents is no exception.

In response to his mother's plan, Jacob raises a practical objection (not a moral one) when he notes that Isaac will surely discover the deception since Esau was so much hairier than Jacob. He worries that if Isaac discovers their plot, his participation will bring down a curse upon him rather than a blessing. Rebekah dismisses his concerns by assuring him that she will bear any curse that falls upon him. To remedy the identity problem, she gives Jacob some of Esau's clothes to wear and puts the skins of the young goats on Jacob's hands and the smooth part of his neck to give him a hairy appearance (at least to someone who is blind).

Genesis tells us what happens:

> So he went in to his father and said, "My father." And he said, "Here I am. Who are you, my son?" Jacob said to his father, "I am Esau your firstborn. I have done as you told me; now sit up and eat of my game, that your soul may bless me." But Isaac said to his son, "How is it that you have found it so quickly, my son?" He answered, "Because the Lord your God granted me success." Then Isaac said to Jacob, "Please come near, that I may feel you, my son, to know whether you are really my son Esau or not." So Jacob went near to Isaac his father, who felt him and said, "The voice is Jacob's voice, but the hands are the hands of Esau." And he did not recognize him, because his hands were hairy like his brother Esau's hands. So he blessed him. He said, "Are you really my son Esau?" He answered, "I am." Then he said, "Bring it near to me, that I may eat of my son's game and bless you."
>
> So he brought it near to him, and he ate; and he brought him wine, and he drank. Then his father Isaac said to him, "Come near and kiss me, my son." So he came near and kissed him. And Isaac smelled the smell of his garments and blessed him and said, "See, the smell of my son is as the smell of a field that the Lord has blessed! May God give you of the dew of heaven and of the fatness of the earth and plenty of grain and wine. Let peoples serve you, and nations bow down to you. Be lord over your brothers, and may your mother's sons bow down to you. Cursed be everyone who curses you, and blessed be everyone who blesses you!" (Genesis 27:18–29)

Isaac apparently has doubts about whether it is Esau that he is speaking to, but through a combination of deceit and lies, Jacob convinces him. His first lie—that he is Esau—leads to a chain of lies as he claims he has killed and cooked an animal. He even brings God into his deception, saying that God granted him quick success in his hunting. For his part, Isaac relies too much on external cues, such as the hairy skin and the smell of the garments, rather than what his mind and heart tell him—that Jacob is attempting to steal his brother's blessing. The phrase in verse 29, "Be lord over your brothers, and may your mother's sons bow down to you," is particularly ironic, as the exact opposite of what Isaac intends occurs. Esau, the older son, will bow down to Jacob, the younger son, as God foretold.

The Aftermath

Isaac quickly and inevitably finds out that he has been duped. As soon as Jacob leaves his father, Esau returns from his hunting trip and brings food to his father. (Jewish legend says that if Jacob had tarried an instant longer in his father's presence, Esau would have discovered the deception and killed him.) When Isaac realizes that Esau is now before him, he "trembled very violently and said, 'Who was it then that hunted game and brought it to me, and I ate it all before you came, and I have blessed him? Yes, and he shall be blessed'" (Genesis 27:33.) Esau is bitterly upset and pleads for his own blessing, saying about his brother, "'Is he not rightly named Jacob ["he cheats"]? For he has cheated me these two times. He took away my birthright, and behold, now he has taken away my blessing'" (Genesis 33:36). Esau seems to have experienced a reversal of feeling—he sold his birthright with casual disregard, yet now he appears to care deeply about the blessing attached to the firstborn son.

Isaac, however, refuses to reverse the blessing, telling Esau that he has already elevated Jacob above him. The

According to a Jewish folktale, "For each blessing invoked upon Jacob by his father Isaac, a similar blessing was bestowed upon him by God himself." This painting of Jacob drawing near to Isaac with a dish of meat was created in the 17th century by Italian artist Bernardo Strozzi.

Bible never gives any reason why Isaac cannot simply revoke Jacob's blessing and bestow it on Esau, other than God's promise that his covenant would be with Jacob rather than Esau. One scholar says, "Isaac could not change his blessings . . . because he knew that the word of God had been fulfilled, just as it had been told to Rebekah." Jewish legend holds that Isaac did not previously know that Esau had sold Jacob his birthright. Upon finding out (after Esau complained about Jacob stealing his blessing), Isaac realizes that Jacob deserved the blessing that went with the birthright and said, "I gave my blessing to the right one!" In any case, there are no stories about Isaac criticizing Jacob.

30 *Jacob*

Isaac refuses to reverse the blessing, even after Esau explains Jacob's deception. Decorative panel from the altar at a German church, circa 1380.

Instead, in the next record of their meeting, Isaac offers additional generous blessings to Jacob.

Esau continues pleading for a blessing, so Isaac answers him with these words, a dubious blessing at best—the first couple of lines are directly opposite of the blessing he gave Jacob: "'Behold, away from the fatness of the earth shall your dwelling be, and away from the dew of heaven on high. By your sword you shall live, and you shall serve your brother; but when you grow restless you shall break his yoke from your neck.'" (Genesis 27:39–40) Later in history, the nation of Edom, which was descended from Esau, fights many times with the nation of Israel, which was descended from Jacob. As the prophecy mentions, Edom even manages to throw off Israelite control several times.

Some argue that Jacob is right to deceive his father in order to gain the blessing. After all, God told Rebekah that Jacob would rule over Esau, and Jacob has already obtained the birthright. All he needs is the final blessing to go along with it, and Isaac's love for Esau is so overwhelming that he is justified in acting on his own initiative to secure the blessing. Others think that Jacob is wrong to deceive his father by taking matters into his own hands that should be left to God. As one scholar says, "All the parties were grievously to blame: Isaac and Esau for planning to reverse the divine decree; Rebekah and Jacob for using the devil's weapons to accomplish God's plan . . . . It was want of faith in God, coupled with the impatience that could not wait till he was ready, that precipitated matters, and gave birth to the lamentable fraud." Indeed, the Bible shows Jacob continually being deceived later in his life, perhaps as a measure of consequence related to his own deception of his father.

The theme of preference being given to the younger brother runs through Israel's history. In the New Testament, the book of Romans says that it is simply God's design to bless Jacob over Esau. There is no favoritism at work, no privilege of birth, but only the grace of God: "And not only so, but also when Rebekah had conceived children by one man, our forefather Isaac, though they were not yet born and had done nothing either good or bad—in order that God's purpose of election might continue, not because of works but because of him who calls—she was told, 'The older will serve the younger.' As it is written, 'Jacob I loved, but Esau I hated.'" (Romans 9:10–13)

JACOB'S PLAN

By now, Esau's dislike of Jacob has turned to full-blown hatred, so much so that he plans to kill Jacob as soon as Isaac dies and the time of mourning is completed. Through an unnamed source (probably one of the household servants), Rebekah catches wind of Esau's plot and tells Jacob to flee to her brother Laban in Haran. The journey serves two purposes. First, it will remove Jacob from Esau's line of fire, as Rebekah told Jacob, "'until your brother's fury turns away . . . and he forgets what you have done to him'" (Genesis 27:44–45). Second, if Jacob leaves Canaan, he'll have the chance to choose a wife from his mother's home country, away from the Canaanite women who caused misery, such as the ones Esau had married (see sidebar). This would be in line with God's desires that his covenant people not mix with the native people of the land. Rebekah even tells Isaac that she hates her life because of the Hittite women that Esau had married. If Jacob does the same, she says, "What good will my life be to me?" (Genesis 27:46).

Rebekah promises Jacob that she will send for him when Esau has cooled down. It turns out that she will

Esau's Wives

When Esau is 40 years old, he marries two Hittite women from the land of Canaan. Genesis 26:35 records that the women make life "bitter" for Isaac and Rebekah—most likely because they are idolatrous foreigners who are outside the bounds of God's covenant relationship with his people. Isaac had chosen Rebekah from among his own people, and his son Esau is now blatantly disregarding the example his godly father had set for him. Esau's character, which is turning out to be opposite of his father's and grandfather's, is becoming increasingly apparent. No other personal details are known about the women he marries, but apparently they do not get along well with their in-laws.

Oddly enough, after seeing Jacob obtain his parents' blessing to seek a non-Canaanite wife in Paddan-aram, Esau attempts to ease their distress and gain their favor by marrying an Ishmaelite relative, one of Abraham's grandchildren, although she was a woman still outside of God's covenant people.

never see her youngest son again—he is away from Canaan for more than 20 years. When Jacob finally returns, Isaac (who feared that he was already close to death before Jacob left) was still alive, but his mother has died. In fact, we are not told anything else about Rebekah in scripture. She probably regrets the situation she finds herself in—her husband seems near death, the son she loves most is gone, her other son probably resents her, and her daughters-in-law make her life miserable. It could be that her circumstances are a result of the curse that she vowed to bear if Jacob were caught deceiving his father.

A Final Blessing

Before Jacob leaves, Isaac adds his instructions to Rebekah's, directing Jacob not to marry a Canaanite woman, but to choose a wife from among the daughters of Laban, his uncle. (Jewish law allowed marriages between first cousins.) He also expands the blessing he gave Jacob earlier, this time explicitly passing down to Jacob God's covenant with Abraham: "'God Almighty bless you and make you fruitful and multiply you, that you may become a company of peoples. May he give the blessing of Abraham to you and to your offspring with you, that you may take possession of the land of your sojournings that God gave to Abraham!'" (Genesis 28:3–4). The name for God that Isaac uses—"God Almighty" from the Hebrew "El Shaddai"—emphasizes God's sovereign power. It is the very name that God himself used when he reaffirmed his covenant with Abraham in Genesis 17. Its use in this case further solidifies Jacob's place in the patriarchy—he is the one who will carry on God's covenant with man.

With that, around 1928 BCE, Jacob is off to Paddan-aram to find a wife and a fortune.

Dreams and Marriage

Jacob departs his family home in Beersheba and heads north toward Haran, venturing on a desperate flight of 850 miles. In stark contrast, Abraham's servant undertook the same journey several decades earlier when he went in search of a bride for Isaac. Abraham's servant traveled with camels, servants, and a flood of gifts. Jacob, on the run for his life, carries a staff in his hand and nothing else. He must have been at least a little afraid to leave behind an angry brother and all he has ever known to strike out for another country. And yet, he must also have had some faith mixed in with his fear—he is acting as he believes God wants him to. Even though he is fleeing the Promised Land, he must have believed that one day he would return to claim the land and the people his father promised would be his. The difficult path of his life, however, requires that he spend time outside of Canaan to mature and become the man

God has called him to be. In marked difference, although his brother Esau never leaves Canaan, he also never lives up to his potential as an heir of a patriarch.

JACOB GLIMPSES GOD

About 50 miles north of Beersheba, at a place he later names Bethel, Jacob stops to spend the night. This location has meaning to Jacob's family, as his grandfather Abraham had been there several times. In fact, God had confirmed his covenant with Abraham and his descendants in that very place. Jacob lies down that night with a stone beneath his head for a pillow—quite a contrast for a man used to having whatever he desired as part of a well-to-do household. As Jacob sleeps, he dreams the first recorded dream in the Bible. In it, he sees a ladder (or a staircase) stretching between earth and heaven, with angels of God ascending and descending upon it. God stands at the top of the ladder and says to Jacob:

> "I am the Lord, the God of Abraham your father and the God of Isaac. The land on which you lie I will give to you and to your offspring. Your offspring shall be like the dust of the earth, and you shall spread abroad to the west and to the east and to the north and to the south, and in you and your offspring shall all the families of the earth be blessed. Behold, I am with you and will keep you wherever you go, and will bring you back to this land. For I will not leave you until I have done what I have promised you." (Genesis 28:13–15)

When Jacob awakens the next morning, he is awed by what he has witnessed. He says: "'Surely the Lord is in this place, and I did not know it. . . . How awesome is this place! This is none other than the house of God, and this is the gate of heaven'" (Genesis 28:16–17). It is no wonder Jacob feels such reverence—this is the first time God has spoken directly to him, and when he does, he confirms that Jacob is the next in line for all three elements of the Abrahamic covenant: land, descendants, and blessing. Based on Jacob's recent actions, he doesn't seem a likely choice as the leader of God's own people, but God still chooses to extend his gracious covenant through him. As he is leaving the country and facing an uncertain future, he must have been particularly reassured by God's promise to bring him back to the only land he has ever known. In the years ahead, he will cling tenaciously to that promise, believing that God will one day bring it to pass. One scholar says the entire episode "was a singularly God-like proceeding, so rich in grace, so comprehensive in its range, so wonderful in its unlimited goodness. It was one of those memorable moments which sometimes occur in the history of good men, when their souls are wrapt in a kind of Elysian balm, as if all God's goodness had been made to pass before them."

The occasion seems so important to Jacob that he follows a common method of the era for marking religious sites. He uses the rock he used as a pillow to make a stone pillar, and then pours oil over it, calling the name of the place Bethel ("house of God"). To seal the consecration, Jacob offers up oil and vows to follow God's covenant, saying, "'If God will be with me and will keep me in this way that I go, and will give me bread to eat and clothing to wear, so that I come again to my father's house in peace, then the Lord shall be my God, and this stone, which I have set up for a pillar, shall be God's house. And of all that you give me I will give a full tenth to you'" (Genesis 28:20–22). He wants to return to his brother's house one day but is not sure if it will happen, so he takes the opportunity to empha-

Jacob's dream of angels ascending and descending between heaven and earth. After awakening, he names the place Bethel, meaning "house of God."

size that point in his vow. He does not yet know what lies in front of him. At the time, says William Blaikie, he "looks for a speedy fulfillment of the divine promise; but as in the case of Abraham and Isaac, a long interval has to pass, and much patience has to be exercised, before the vision of faith is turned into the reality of experience."

Jacob even pledges to give a tenth of whatever he earns back to God as a tithe. This was not a command of God, but is already known and practiced by some as an acknowledgement of God's blessing. As one scholar says, "Jacob may have been bargaining with God, as if to buy His favor rather than purely worshipping God with his gift, but it is best to . . . see Jacob's vow and offering as genuine worship based on confidence in God's promise."

Scripture makes no mention of it, but Jewish legend holds that during Jacob's journey to Haran, Esau sends his son Eliphaz to intercept and kill him. Eliphaz catches up to Jacob, but Jacob talks him out of killing him; when Eliphaz returns to his father, Esau is so angry that he pursues Jacob himself and would have killed him if not for timely interventions from God.

Jacob in Haran

Jewish legend also says that Jacob's journey to Haran is made easier by five successive miracles. The first miracle is that the sun sinks as he passes Mount Moriah, causing him to stop and spend the night in the spot where God wants to reveal himself in a dream. In the second miracle, Jacob takes 12 stones from the altar where his father had once lain. The 12 stones fuse into one stone (the one Jacob uses as a pillow), signifying that Jacob is to become

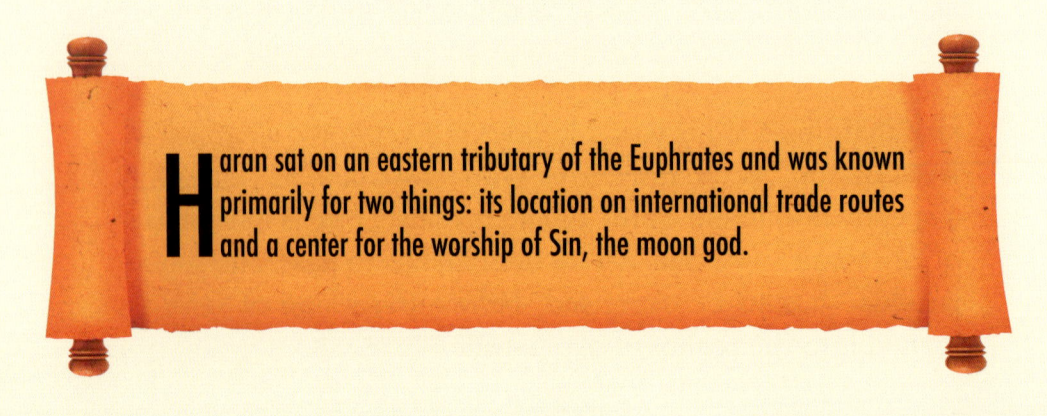

Haran sat on an eastern tributary of the Euphrates and was known primarily for two things: its location on international trade routes and a center for the worship of Sin, the moon god.

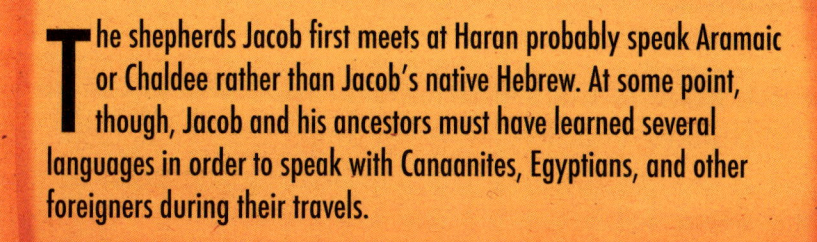

> The shepherds Jacob first meets at Haran probably speak Aramaic or Chaldee rather than Jacob's native Hebrew. At some point, though, Jacob and his ancestors must have learned several languages in order to speak with Canaanites, Egyptians, and other foreigners during their travels.

the father of the 12 tribes of Israel. In the third miracle (which has only happened four times in history, according to the legend), the earth jumps from Mount Moriah to Haran, allowing Jacob to arrive in the twinkling of an eye. The last two miracles come in the course of his introduction to Haran.

When Jacob first arrives in Haran, the "land of the people of the east" (Genesis 29:1), he encounters several shepherds gathered with their flocks of sheep around a well in a field. (It is possible that Rebekah had told him of a likely gathering spot where he could make contact with his relatives.) A large stone lies over the mouth of the well, most likely to protect the scarce water inside from evaporation, contamination, and unlawful use. Jacob asks the shepherds if they know Laban. They say that they do and that Laban's daughter Rachel is on her way to the well to water her flocks. Jacob tries to convince the men to water their sheep quickly and leave, but they say they must wait until Rachel arrives so they can water their sheep at the same time.

When Rachel, who is a shepherdess (the only woman with that job description in the Bible), arrives, Jacob (the nonphysical twin who would rather sit indoors than work outside) quickly comes near and rolls the stone away from the mouth of the well so her flocks—and the others—could drink. This is a difficult job—in fact, Jewish legend says the superhuman strength necessary to move such a great stone is the fourth miracle that aids Jacob. In the fifth and final miracle, water automatically rises from deep in the well to the very top, eliminating the need to draw the water up by hand. The legend says that the water remains at the top of the well the entire 20 years that Jacob spends in Haran. Jewish legend also holds that "to meet young maidens on first entering a city is a sure sign that fortune is favorable to one's undertakings." If so, Jacob is well on his way to big things, for he has just met the woman who will become his wife.

As her flocks begin to drink, Jacob kisses Rachel in the custom of the time. Watering and kissing might not seem to be related, but in this case they are. "Their parallel nature is clear in the Hebrew, in which the words 'he watered' and 'he kissed' have the same consonants," says one scholar. "One might almost say that his mouth watered equally at the sight of Laban's daughter and of his flocks." Jacob weeps aloud and tells Rachel that he is her father's kinsman and the son of her aunt Rebekah. It has been 97 years since Rebekah has left, so her family is anxious for news. Rachel runs to tell her father of Jacob's presence; Laban in turn then runs to meet Jacob and bring him to his house, saying, "'Surely you are my bone and my flesh!'" (Genesis 29:14).

Romance

The tradition of the time allowed strangers to stay in a home for three days. On the fourth day, the visitor had to disclose his name and purpose for being there. The stranger could remain longer if he or she worked out an agreement with the host for a job and wages. Jacob stays

Jacob kisses Rachel at the well, as described in Genesis 29:11.

with Laban a month before Laban broaches the subject and asks what Jacob would like his wages to be. This story says that Laban has another daughter, Leah, who is Rachel's older sister. The Bible says that Leah's eyes are weak or soft (this could mean that they are a pale color—which would have been looked on as a blemish—rather than the sparkling, dark eyes that were common), but Rachel was "beautiful in form and appearance" (Genesis 29:17). The very next verse simply says, "Jacob loved Rachel" (Genesis 29:18). Given that love, he tells Laban that he will work seven years for the privilege of marrying Rachel. Laban responds that he would rather give Rachel to Jacob than to anyone else, so Jacob serves his seven years, "and they seemed to him but a few days because of the love he had for her" (Genesis 29:20). The historian Josephus says, "But Jacob was quite overcome, not so much by their kindred, nor by that affection which might arise thence, as by his love to the damsel, and his surprise at her beauty, which was so flourishing, as few of the women of that age could vie with."

Jacob is probably close to 50 years old by the time he begins working for Laban. He has never known physical labor like this before, but he has never been in love like this before, either. The language the Bible uses to describe their relationship is quite romantic. Jacob and Rachel have a genuine love built not just on physical attraction, but through friendship and getting to know each other over time. The immediate attraction they had for one another brings to mind Isaac's romance with Rebekah so many years before. Jacob's spiritual character is softening as well—he is no longer trying to deceive anyone but is working hard to attain the desire of his heart.

THE BIG SWITCH

His past deceptions do come back to haunt him, though, and he ends up on the wrong end of a deception, the consequences of which reverberate throughout the rest of his life. At the end of the agreed-upon seven years, Laban throws a wedding party complete with a feast to celebrate Jacob's marriage. In the evening, however, without Jacob's knowledge, he switches brides and gives his older daughter Leah to Jacob instead of Rachel. Jacob spends the night with her and "in the morning, behold, it was Leah!" (Genesis 29:25). Jacob goes straight to the mastermind of the scheme and says, "'What is this you have done to me? Did I not serve you for Rachel? Why then have you deceived me?'" (Genesis 29:25). Laban replies that in his country, the oldest daughter has to be given away before the younger. He offers to give Rachel to Jacob as a wife after the week of celebration of his marriage to Leah is

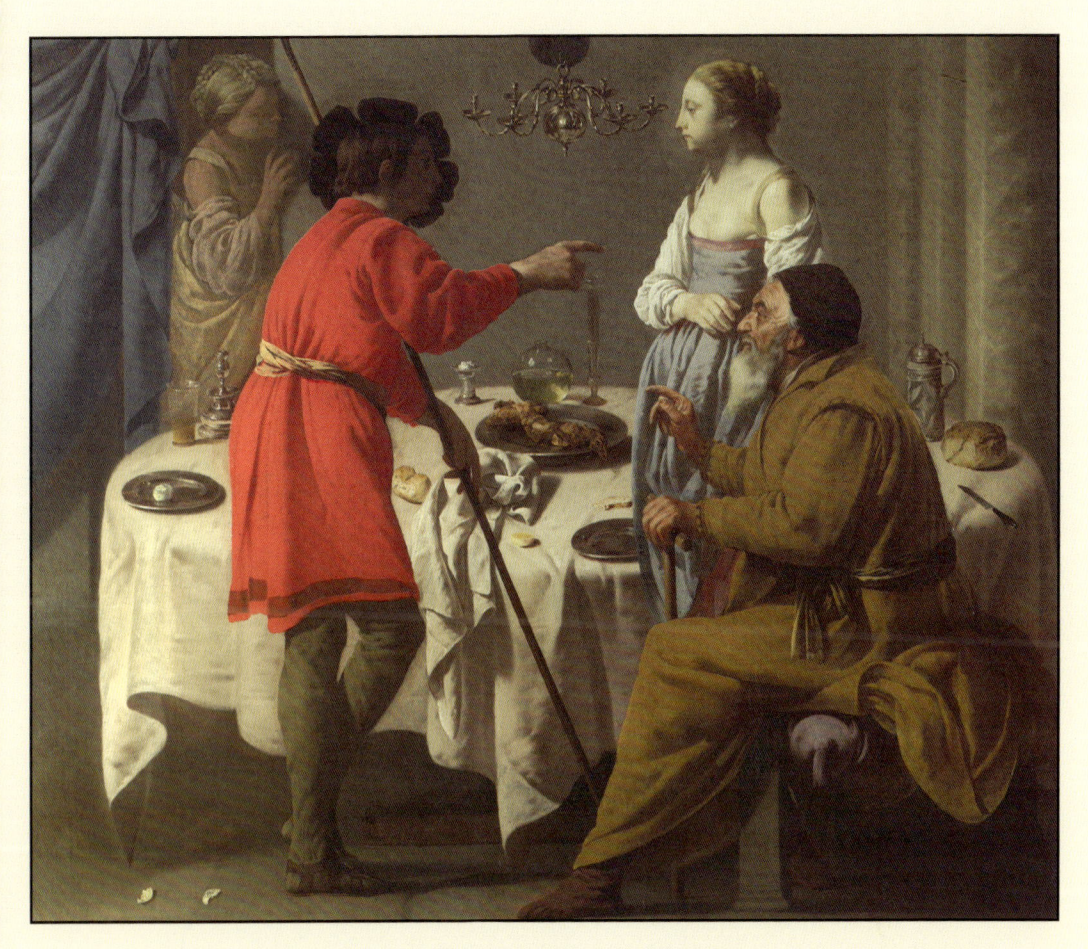

Jacob confronts Laban after his marriage to Leah. This painting by the Dutch master Hendrick ter Brugghen was completed in 1627.

finished, with the stipulation that Jacob will then serve Laban another seven years for Rachel. Polygamy was common in those times, although against God's prescription for men. It was later forbidden by Mosaic Law.

Several questions spring to mind after reading this account. Perhaps first and foremost is how Laban could pull off a switch like this. It seems inconceivable that such a thing could happen, and yet it does. Leah probably wears a heavy veil during the actual wedding ceremony, keeping Jacob from seeing her face clearly. Later, as Jacob and his new wife head for their wedding chamber, a Jewish Midrash says all the guests extinguish their candles, leaving everything dark (their explanation to Jacob was that their culture was more modest than Jacob's was). Josephus adds that Jacob was "both in drink and the dark." In that case, he would not have discovered the switch until the morning light dawned.

Even though this is Laban's scheme, he needs help principally from Leah, who deceives Jacob when he calls for Rachel that night. Rachel, presumably, is coerced into going along with the plan or is restrained in some way by Laban, for surely she wants to stop the deception. The Testament of Issachar records Rachel telling Leah, "You are not his [true] wife, it was only by trickery that you were taken to him in my place. My father tricked me and replaced me that night, not permitting Jacob to see me. If I had been there, this would not have happened" (Testament of Issachar 1:10–13).

Why would Laban pull a scam of such consequence? He claims the firstborn daughter has to be married first. But if that is the case, why does he not inform Jacob of this earlier? Some commentators believe it is because Leah is not as attractive as her younger sister (as signified by the phrase "soft eyes") and so Laban has to rely on deceit to marry her off. "Laban carried out this trickery in part because of Leah's unattractiveness, for during the seven years of Rachel's betrothal, no one had come to marry her [Leah]." Jewish legend says Laban manipulated events in order to gain another seven years of work from Jacob.

Whatever the reason, Jacob's scheming ways have finally come back to haunt him. Even in his righteous anger at Laban, says Blaikie, "amid all Jacob's irritation and indignation at this miserable fraud, one consideration

The Veiling

A veil is not a requirement in modern Jewish weddings, but for those who choose to wear one, the potential problem of marrying the wrong woman has been remedied. According to Rabbi Telushkin, "At Jewish weddings today, a procedure called the ba-deh-kin, at which the groom personally veils the bride before the ceremony, ensures that the groom's new father-in-law has not slipped in any substitutes."

A more romantic interpretation of the custom says that by obscuring his bride's face with a veil, the groom is declaring that he loves her for more than her outward beauty.

---

would tend to calm him—it was just the treatment and the trick he had practised on his father. It is often seen that those who use craft and cunning as their weapons find themselves, like Shakespeare's engineers, 'hoist on their own petard,' through similar deceptions practised on them by others."

One final anecdote from Jewish legend sums up the situation nicely. The morning after Jacob is deceived, he bitterly rebukes Leah for what she has done. "O thou deceiver," he says, "daughter of a deceiver, why didst thou answer me when I called Rachel's name?" Leah responds: "Is there a teacher without a pupil? I but profited by thy instruction. When thy father called thee Esau, didst thou not say, 'Here am I'?" Jacob has been sorely deceived in a bitterly unfair manner, yet he has to realize he is still reaping the consequences of all the deception he previously practiced in his life. As one scholar says, "There is an ironic fitness in Laban's deception. Jacob's reach for the rights of the firstborn son got him the firstborn daughter as well."

5

BUILDING A FAMILY AND A FORTUNE

Jacob only wanted to marry one woman. He now has four women in his life: two wives and their maids. He loves Rachel more than Leah—she is, after all, the one he wanted to marry—but this favoritism, however understandable, will lead to untold misery.

THE CHILDBEARING YEARS

Leah, of course, senses that Jacob does not love her. She probably had not fully thought through all the implications of her actions when she agreed to take part in Laban's trickery; she has gained a husband, but at what price? He does not love her. The term "not loved" or "hated" also has legal connotations that show Leah's insecure position. In that culture, she was the unfavorite wife, which means she was in danger of being divorced. The situation leads to an intense competition between the two sisters for the affections of their husband. The rivalry manifests itself primarily in childbearing, and it is here that Leah has the edge. She finds that she can easily bear children for Jacob, while Rachel remains barren—a fate as dreaded as death in the ancient Near East culture. Each sister then, has one area in which she excels and one large problem that brings her grief. Rachel is loved by Jacob, but cannot bear children. Leah can bear children, but is not loved. The Bible reader can trace the ups and downs of their competition for the heart of their husband through the children they (and their maids) bear and the names they give those children.

Scripture records that God opens Leah's womb specifically because she is unloved. Leah perhaps places too much hope in this; when her first son Reuben (meaning "see, a son") is born, she says, "'Because the Lord has looked upon my affliction; for now my husband will love me'" (Genesis 29:32). When she gives birth to her second son, Simeon ("heard"), she says, "'Because the Lord has heard that I am hated, he has given me this son also'" (Genesis 29:33). Her status has not changed by the time her third son is due, so she names him Levi ("attached") in the hopes that "'this time my husband will be attached to me, because I have borne him three sons'" (Genesis 29:34). By the time she produces a fourth son, she apparently realizes that children will not automatically bring the love and attention she so desires, so she shifts her focus from Jacob to God and names her son Judah ("praise"), saying, "'This time I will praise the Lord'" (Genesis 29:35). After her fourth son is born, Leah stops bearing children for a time.

Rachel watches her sister produce child after child, growing more envious with each successive birth. She vents to Jacob (in a request that unfortunately becomes true later in her life), "'Give me children or I die!'" (Genesis 30:1). Jacob in turn becomes angry and fires

Leah and her children. Detail from a fresco by Giovanni Tiepolo, circa 1700.

back: "'Am I in the place of God, who has withheld from you the fruit of the womb?'" (Genesis 30:2). Even though he is angry with her, he still believes that God controls all aspects of their lives, including the birth of children. Rachel then hits upon a solution through a common practice of the day. She offers her maid Bilhah to Jacob so that she can bear surrogate children for Rachel. In this way, a wife could provide a child to her husband—the surrogate mother would give birth while actually sitting on the knees of the wife. Bilhah then gives birth to Dan ("judged"), for Rachel says, "'God has judged me and has also heard my voice and given me a son'" (Genesis 30:6). Bilhah later has a second son, whom Rachel calls Naphtali ("wrestling")—a specific reference to the conflict with her sister. She says, "'With mighty wrestlings I have wrestled with my sister and have prevailed'" (Genesis 30:8).

When Leah realizes that Rachel is surging in the competition while she has plateaued, she gives her own maid, Zilpah, to Jacob in the same manner as Rachel had. Zilpah becomes pregnant and bears a son whom Leah calls Gad ("good fortune"), saying, "'Good fortune has come!'" (Genesis 30:11). Zilpah then gives birth to yet another son, whom Leah names Asher ("happy"), saying, "'Happy am I! For women have called me happy'" (Genesis 30:13).

By this time, Jacob has been married about six years and fathered eight sons with three different women. When his firstborn son, Reuben, is about five years old, he finds some small, orange-colored, tomato-shaped fruits called mandrakes in a wheat field and brings them to his mother, Leah. Her sister Rachel catches sight of them and asks if she may have a few. She most likely thinks they will enable her to conceive, for mandrakes, or "love apples," were used as an aphrodisiac and were thought to promote fertility. Rachel's scheme backfires, though, as Leah drives a hard bargain: She will give the mandrakes to

Illustration of mandrake root, from a 1795 botanical treatise. In Hebrew, the word mandrake *means "love plant" or "love apple." In many cultures throughout history, mandrake roots have been considered to have magical powers—perhaps because the roots can resemble the human form. However, mandrake should not be ingested, as all parts of the plant and root are poisonous.*

Rachel in exchange for Jacob spending the night with her (apparently, he normally lives with Rachel). Here is another sign that all is not well between the sisters and that they are still in conflict with one another as Leah says in response to Rachel's request, "'Is it a small matter that you have taken away my husband? Would you take away my son's mandrakes also?'" (Genesis 30:15).

As a result of the trade, Leah gives birth to another son, whom she names Issachar ("wages" or "hire"), saying, "'God has given me my wages because I gave my servant to my husband'" (Genesis 30:18). She then bears Jacob's 10th son, naming him Zebulon ("honor"), for she says, "'God has endowed me with a good endowment; now my husband will honor me, because I have borne him six sons'" (Genesis 30:20). And after all the boys, she gives birth to a daughter named Dinah, who will play a significant role later in Jacob's life.

Finally, it is Rachel's turn. After seven years of waiting and pleading and crying, the Bible says that "God remembered Rachel, and God listened to her and opened her womb" (Genesis 30:22). She bears a son and names him

Consequences of the Mandrakes

Jewish legend disapproves of Rachel's mandrake deal with Leah, calling it "unbecoming conduct . . . to dispose thus of her husband." As a consequence, the legend goes, Rachel gains the mandrakes but later gives birth to only two sons, rather than the four she would have if she had not traded away her husband. The legend also says she loses the privilege to rest in a grave beside him. She is the only matriarch or patriarch not buried in the Cave of Machpelah at Hebron.

Joseph ("may he add"), saying, "'May the Lord add to me another son!'" (Genesis 30:24).

Despite this note of happiness for Rachel, these years cannot have been happy for this dysfunctional family. While polygamy was common in that culture and time, it always caused problems. This family's troubles feature a rivalry between sisters, anger and grief over barrenness, a childbearing competition, bargaining for time with a shared husband, surrogate mothers, and lots of children—so far, the births of 11 boys and 1 girl have been recorded. It did not have to be this way for Jacob's family. God had promised at Bethel that he would be with Jacob and his family, and that he would keep him and bring him back to the land of promise. Jacob, Rachel, and Leah were heirs to this promise, but they did not live in light of it—they squandered an opportunity to live above their struggles. And yet, through all the difficulty, God does not abandon his promise. He is only mentioned briefly in this section of the account of Jacob's life, but the birth of Jacob's children marks the beginning of the line of descendants that will lead to the future King David.

JACOB AND LABAN

Having established Jacob's family situation, the biblical narrative turns to Jacob's business dealings with his father-in-law. Jacob has worked hard for Laban for seven years that flew by as he anticipated his marriage to Rachel. The second seven years pass more slowly, but Jacob is still diligent—when the mandrake episode is described, the narrative says he comes in from the field in the evening, meaning that he had been working outside all day. Now that Rachel has at last given birth, Jacob feels free to pursue the possibility of returning to his own home and country. He approaches Laban and tells him he has fulfilled his service to him and he wants to return to his home country. Laban has prospered while Jacob has been with him and he does not like the idea of Jacob leaving, so he bargains with him. First, he tells Jacob he knows God has blessed him and his household because of Jacob's presence, and then he asks Jacob what his wages should be. Jacob responds by reminding Laban of the good he has done him: "'For you had little before I came, and it has increased abundantly, and the Lord has blessed you wherever I turned'" (Genesis 30:30). Jacob's faithful work has evidently paid off to the benefit of his father-in-law with increased flocks, herds and grain production.

Laban again asks how he can convince Jacob to stay, and Jacob answers with what seems like a strange proposition:

> "You shall not give me anything. If you will do this for me, I will again pasture your flock and keep it: let me pass through all your flock today, removing from it every speckled and spotted sheep and every black lamb, and the spotted and speckled among the goats, and they shall be my wages. So my honesty will answer for me later, when you come to look into my wages with you. Every one that is not speckled and spotted among the goats and black among the lambs, if found with me, shall be counted stolen." (Genesis 30:31–33)

Laban agrees and then promptly removes from his flocks all male and female goats that were striped, speckled, and spotted, along with every lamb that has black on it, depositing them all three days' journey from Jacob. His true nature has revealed itself again: Laban is a habitual deceiver.

Laban's nature is revealed back in Genesis 24, when Abraham's servant came in search of a bride for Isaac,

Jacob and Laban come to an agreement on Jacob's wages. Jewish legend holds that Rachel had warned Jacob about her father's deceptive nature even before their wedding, saying, "My father is cunning, and thou art not his match."

bringing many gifts. Almost the first thing we are told about Laban (Rebekah's brother) is that he notices the ring and bracelets Abraham's servant had given Rebekah. It is a small detail, perhaps, but it shows where his heart is. His eyes do not go directly to Rebekah to make sure she is okay after a meeting with a strange man; instead, he looks first at the jewelry the obviously rich man had brought. That same spirit of striving for earthly gain in whatever manner possible is a recurring theme with Laban. He has a habit of not telling the truth. He switches daughters at Jacob's wedding and by doing so, squeezes another seven years of work out of Jacob. One Jewish scholar maintains that ever since Laban's deception at the wedding, Jewish tradition has labeled him as "the personification of an evil and manipulative man."

Laban is no model employer either. He seems to keep Jacob around mostly for his own benefit—he gets a hard worker, plus he is growing wealthier, for he realizes that God is with Jacob, blessing whatever he does. Jewish legend says that Laban's household gods realize this as soon as Jacob comes to Haran, and they advise Laban to employ Jacob, saying, "Beware of sending him away from thy house. His star and his constellation are so lucky that good fortune will attend all his undertakings, and for his sake the blessing of the Lord will rest upon all thou doest, in thy house or in thy field." Their counsel gives Laban even more incentive to squeeze all he can out of Jacob while giving him as little in return as possible, no matter how hard Jacob works. He also has a habit of lying. The biblical narrative reveals later that he changes Jacob's wages 10 times; Jewish legend says Laban changes their agreement 100 times and is an "archvillain . . . whose tongue wagged in all directions, and who made all sorts of promises that were never kept, judged others by himself, and therefore suspected Jacob of wanting to deceive him. And yet, in the end, it was Laban himself who broke his word."

As another scholar says, Jacob has come to find Laban "a most uncomfortable master. There was no reliance to be placed on him nor on his promises . . . a careful and skillful man among cattle, he had been the means of greatly increasing Laban's stock, making him now a rich man compared to what he was. Laban . . . had that shabby way of doing things, that if a servant was once in his power he would prevent him from getting away, or from doing anything to better his situation."

Now, faced with an admittedly odd business proposal, Laban does the first thing he thinks of—he cheats just to make sure he is getting the better end of the bargain.

JACOB'S PROSPERITY

Jacob, however, has finally caught on to Laban's deceptions and is prepared for them. He has spent more than 14 years studying Laban's flocks (plus all his years with his father's animals) and he has used his time wisely, for he knows how to breed the sheep in a manner that benefits him. He sets out upon a strange breeding program to increase his wealth (measured primarily in flocks and herds rather than money). He peels white streaks in fresh sticks of poplar and almond and plane trees and sets the sticks in front of the watering troughs where the flocks come to drink. The sheep and goats tend to breed when they came to drink, so in Jacob's program, they breed in front of the sticks and produce striped, speckled, and spotted offspring. When he sees the stronger animals of the flocks breeding, he lays the

A modern shepherd leads his flock through the desert to find pasture in Israel.

peeled sticks in the troughs; when the feebler animals breed, he packs the sticks away. When the offspring are born, he faithfully separates out his flocks from Laban's in accord with their agreement. The method works well for Jacob: "Thus the man increased greatly and had large flocks, female servants and male servants, and camels and donkeys" (Genesis 30:43).

So why does this breeding program work? It probably has to do with a combination of sound genetic principles that Jacob had learned and some beliefs that were not as scientific. Jacob knows from experience that when a speckled or spotted animal is born, he can breed that particular beast selectively in order to produce more marked animals (the recessive gene that causes the markings is being passed down). These animals are not physically inferior; they just have a few markings on their coats. Once he has this part of his program running, Jacob tries to increase the output with the peeled sticks. An age-old belief says that "sensory impressions at the moment of conception affect the embryo." Here, the strips of white against dark bark would cause spots or markings in the offspring.

Another explanation is that Jacob had learned that when the bark was peeled, it released a sexual stimulant into the water that encouraged the animals to breed. In Genesis 30:38, the word bred in Hebrew literally means to be hot, as when animals are "in heat." Others believe that God simply told Jacob what to do and he did it. Says one scholar, "The good man [Jacob] did not do this of his own devising, but because divine grace inspired his mind [to do so]. For, you see, it was not done on the basis of any human reasoning, since it was quite extraordinary and beyond the grasp of logic." However it came about, the plan works, and Jacob becomes wealthier as time passes.

6

RETURN TO CANAAN

Over the next six years, Jacob prospers so much that Laban's sons become jealous and suspicious of him, saying, "'Jacob has taken all that was our father's, and from what was our father's he has gained all this wealth'" (Genesis 31:1). Jacob and Laban both hear these complaints, and Laban joins his sons in resenting Jacob's success. He doesn't have a problem with Jacob's work when it benefits him, but when the benefits begin accruing in Jacob's favor, he grows angry. For his part, Jacob is aware that Laban's attitude has changed so that he no longer regards Jacob in a positive light.

With agreeably good timing, God speaks to Jacob, saying, "'Return to the land of your fathers and to your kindred, and I will be with you'" (Genesis 31:3). God invokes his covenant language—"land of your fathers" and "I will be with you"—to encourage Jacob to leave. Jacob needs to discuss his plans with his wives away from anyone who might carry a report back to Laban, so he calls Rachel and Leah into the field where he tends to his flocks. Once there, he tells them of their father's change in attitude toward him and he presents his case for leaving their homeland. He says that God has been with him and he has served Laban with all his strength, even as Laban continually changed his wages. He gives God credit for watching over him and prospering him, saying that God had told him in a dream that he was causing the flocks to produce striped, spotted, and mottled animals as a recompense for Laban's treatment of him. In the same dream, God confirmed that Jacob was to leave, saying, "'I am the God of Bethel, where you anointed a pillar and made a vow to me. Now arise, go out from this land and return to the land of your kindred'" (Genesis 31:13).

Rachel and Leah are all for the plan. They know their father now has no inheritance for them and even regards them as foreigners because they married Jacob. "For he has sold us and he has indeed devoured our money,'" they

Jacob's Protection

Jewish legend says that Jacob has two hosts of 600,000 angels watching over him as he leaves Haran—one to protect him to the borders of Canaan, and the other to watch over him in the Holy Land, especially as he confronts his brother Esau.

Despite the angels, Jacob knows he cannot hope to defeat 400 men if his brother orders his army to attack, so he turns to other methods. Jewish legend says that he has three means to save himself: "He would cry to God for help, appease Esau's wrath with presents, and hold himself in readiness for war if the worst came to the worst."

This 17th century Neapolitan painting depicts Jacob and his family leaving Laban's home to journey to Canaan.

said. "'All the wealth that God has taken away from our father belongs to us and to our children. Now then, whatever God has said to you, do,'" (Genesis 31:15–16).

Jacob decides that he needs to leave town quickly and quietly, although with 2 wives, 11 children, numerous servants, and countless possessions and animals (Jewish legend says that Jacob left Haran with 600,000 in his herds), that will not be an easy task. He does not inform Laban that he is leaving; instead, he picks a time when he knows Laban is out shearing sheep, probably at his flock three days away. Shearing, says Robert Alter, was "a very elaborate procedure involving large numbers of men, and accompanied by feasting, and so would have provided an excellent cover for Jacob's flight." While Laban is gone, Jacob "fled with all that he had and arose and crossed the

Four bronze Canaanite idols, ca. 2000 BCE. In the pagan culture of the ancient Middle East, small figurines like these were thought to bring prosperity to their owners by ensuring that fields were productive and livestock fertile.

Euphrates, and set his face toward the hill country of Gilead" (Genesis 31:21).

As they leave, Rachel steals her father's household gods, which were usually small figures of goddesses representing the deities responsible for protecting the household and promoting its prosperity and fertility. It is unclear why Rachel steals them. Her former way of worship (before she married Jacob, who worshiped the one true God) could still be a part of her life, or she may be taking them as a bargaining chip in case Laban catches up with them.

Jacob moves quickly at first in order to put as much ground between himself and Laban as possible before Laban discovers that he is gone. He probably packs up and heads out fairly rapidly, falling into a particular order of march with all his goods and people, as one scholar describes:

> The tents are quickly struck, and, together with all the movables and possessions, packed on the backs of camels, or mules, or asses, and the whole party will very quickly be on its way, leaving not a rag or halter behind. The order of march in the removal of a pastoral tribe or family seems to be . . . the sheep and goats usually lead the van, and are followed by the camels, perhaps asses, laden more or less with the property of the community, consisting of the tents, with their cordage, mats, carpets, clothes, skins, water and provision bags, boilers and pots, and sundry other utensils, bundled up in admirable confusion,— unless when all the property belongs to one person, as in the case of Jacob. The laden beasts are usually followed by the elderly men, the women and the children, who are mostly on foot in the ordinary migrations with the flocks . . . the very young children are carried on the backs or in the arms of their mothers, who in general are on foot, but are sometimes mounted with their infants on the spare or lightly-laden beasts . . . the chief himself brings up the rear, accompanied by the principal persons of the party . . . it would seem as if most of Jacob's people went on foot; it is only said that he set his wives and children upon camels.

LABAN CATCHES JACOB

It is three days before Laban finds out that Jacob and his family are gone. He immediately takes his kinsmen and leaves, traveling fast and light in an effort to catch Jacob.

Even so, it takes a full week of pursuit until he overtakes Jacob in the hill country of Gilead. The night before Laban meets with Jacob, God appears to Laban in a dream and cautions him to speak nothing good or bad to Jacob in an effort to bring him back to Haran.

When Laban finally faces Jacob, he asks several questions:

> "What have you done, that you have tricked me and driven away my daughters like captives of the sword? Why did you flee secretly and trick me, and did not tell me, so that I might have sent you away with mirth and songs, with tambourine and lyre? And why did you not permit me to kiss my sons and my daughters farewell? Now you have done foolishly . . . and now you have gone away because you longed greatly for your father's house, but why did you steal my gods?" (Genesis 31:26–30).

Laban does not believe that his daughters have left willingly with Jacob, and he is understandably upset that he did not get to say goodbye to his daughters and grandchildren. Given his character, it is difficult to determine how much of what he says is true.

Jacob tells Laban that he left so quickly because he was afraid Laban would forcefully take his daughters

---

Jacob must have had a large number of servants to watch over in addition to his own family and his flocks and herds. Abraham was also wealthy, and Genesis 14:14 records that he had at least 318 trained men (servants or bodyguards) who were part of his household.

Laban searches for his idols among Jacob's possessions. It is remarkable how easily Rachel slips into the pattern of deception that has marked her husband and her father. As one scholar says, "Rachel was a fitting wife for Jacob and a fitting daughter for Laban, craftier than both of them."

back from Jacob. He also proclaims that anyone found with Laban's gods will die—he does not know that Rachel has stolen them. The gods are tremendously important to Laban; he makes a thorough search of the tent belonging to Jacob, Rachel, Leah, and the two female servants, but does not find them. Rachel has hidden the idols in her camel's saddle and tells her father that she cannot get up to let him search because "'the way of women is upon me'" (Genesis 31:35).

Deception is proving to be a family talent. Rachel's theft and lies indicate that her trust in God is not yet complete—even after 20 years of marriage to Jacob, the heir to God's covenant, she has not fully given herself to that covenant. Jacob's harsh, impulsive words concerning the fate of the one who stole the idols could be construed to find their fulfillment in Rachel's premature death during the birth of Benjamin, her second son.

COVENANT OF PEACE

When Laban comes away with nothing from his search, Jacob lets 20 years of frustration toward Laban burst forth. He says:

> "What is my offense? What is my sin, that you have hotly pursued me? For you have felt through all my goods; what have you found of all your household goods? Set it here before my kinsmen and your kinsmen, that they may decide between us two. These twenty years I have been with you. Your ewes and your female goats have not miscarried, and I have not eaten the rams of your flocks. What was torn by wild beasts I did not bring to you. I bore the loss of it myself. From my hand you required it, whether stolen by day or stolen by night. There I was: by day the heat consumed me, and the cold by night, and my sleep fled from my eyes. These twenty years I have been in your house. I served you fourteen years for your two daughters, and six years for your flock, and you have changed my wages ten times. If the God of my father, the God of Abraham and the Fear of Isaac, had not been on my side, surely now you would have sent me away empty-handed. God saw my affliction and the labor of my hands and rebuked you last night." (Genesis 31:36–42)

His speech fills in a few of the details from his time in Haran, showing that he was an intelligent, sacrificial, and diligent employee of his father-in-law, even when that father-in-law treated him poorly. As one scholar says, "In exile, the 'slippery man' of Canaan was learning to be a 'blameless man.'" Laban weakly says that all that Jacob had was his own, but his argument does not amount to much, and Laban takes nothing of what Jacob had brought with him.

The two men decide to conclude their relationship with a covenant that will be a witness between them; they erect a pile of stones that Jacob calls Galeed ("the heap of witness") and eat together. Laban reminds Jacob that God will be a witness if he mistreats Leah or Rachel or takes another wife besides them. Both men agreed that they would not pass beyond the stone pile to do each other harm; Laban swears by the God of Abraham and Nahor (his own grandfather), while Jacob swears by the fear of his father Isaac (which tells us that Isaac put a high premium on the fear of

In the ancient Middle East of Jacob's time, so-called "standing stones" (in Hebrew, masseboth, "to stand up") were erected to mark treaties or agreements, or to commemorate important events. The Bible records four cases in which Jacob erects a massebah: after his dream at Bethel (Genesis 28:18-22), when he leaves Laban (Genesis 31:51-53), when he returns to Bethel (Genesis 35:14-15), and at Rachel's grave near Bethlehem (Genesis 35:19). This example of a standing stone is located in modern-day Israel.

God). As the priest of his family, Jacob offers a sacrifice to God, and they all share a meal together.

The covenant gives Jacob and Laban a chance to part, if not as friends, at least not as enemies. Neither can really enforce the covenant because they will live so far apart, but they officially have made peace. The next morning, Laban arises early, kisses and blesses his daughters and grandchildren, and returns home. Laban's departure marks the last known contact between Abraham's descendants in Canaan and his relatives in Mesopotamia.

Entering Canaan

Jacob and his family are at last headed home. He is a far different man than 20 years before. He trusts that God is going to fulfill his covenant relationship with him, and he has found love, children, wealth and a surprising amount of character tempered by trial and responsibility. Life in Canaan awaits him, but he first must deal with his estranged brother Esau. As Jacob's caravan begins moving again, Jacob sends messengers ahead to Esau. Even though he has been gone for 20 years, he knows Esau will not have forgotten the circumstances under which he left—Jacob had embarrassed and humiliated his brother by tricking their father into giving him the firstborn blessing, leaving Esau in a murderous rage. Rather than be surprised by Esau, he sends a message for him with his couriers: "Thus says your servant Jacob, 'I have sojourned with Laban and stayed until now. I have oxen, donkeys, flocks, male servants, and female servants. I have sent to tell my lord, in order that I may find favor in your sight'" (Genesis 32:5). The message is carefully designed to show no threat; Jacob acts as Esau's servant and lets him know he has plenty of his own possessions so he is not returning to conquer everything Esau owns. Nevertheless, the messengers return to Jacob with news that frightens him: Esau has heard the message and is coming to meet Jacob along with 400 men. To Jacob, this confirms that Esau not only remembers his anger, but it has not abated—he is coming to wipe Jacob off the face of the earth.

Even though Jacob is "greatly afraid and distressed" (Genesis 32:7), he begins thinking strategically. He divides his people, flocks, herds, and camels into two camps, reasoning that if Esau attacks one camp, the other will be free to escape. Jacob then prays for the first recorded time since he prayed at Bethel on the way to Haran. He says:

> "O God of my father Abraham and God of my father Isaac, O Lord who said to me, 'Return to your country and to your kindred, that I may do you good,' I am not worthy of the least of all the deeds of steadfast love and all the faithfulness that you have shown to your servant, for with only my staff I crossed this Jordan, and now I have become two camps. Please deliver me from the hand of my brother, from the hand of Esau, for I fear him, that he may come and attack me, the mothers with the children. But you said, 'I will surely do you good, and make your offspring as the sand of the sea, which cannot be numbered for multitude.'" (Genesis 32:10–12)

It is a remarkable prayer, for Jacob admits his fear and reminds God of his covenant promise to him, humbly asking for help. His humility shows how far he has come from his younger days when he forcibly took whatever he wanted. His statement, "I am not worthy of the least of all the deeds of steadfast love and all the faithfulness that you have shown to your servant," shows that he fully realizes his own unworthiness and dependence on God's grace.

Jacob's reliance on God for protection does not mean that he abandons his responsibility to care for his family, so he sets about making even more plans to dissuade Esau from attacking him. He gathers together an enormously vast gift for Esau, including "two hundred female goats and twenty male goats, two hundred ewes and twenty rams, thirty milking camels and their calves, forty cows and ten bulls, twenty female donkeys and ten male donkeys" (Genesis 32:14–15)—a total of 550 animals. If Jacob can spare a gift that large for his brother, he is truly wealthy, for only a man with vast reserves in store would give such a gift.

Jacob instructs his servants to pass ahead of him and take the animals to Esau, leaving some space between each group of animals. When Esau asked who they were and who the animals belonged to, they were to answer, "They belong to your servant Jacob. They are a present sent to my lord Esau. And moreover, he is behind us" (Genesis 32:18). Jacob reasons that the presents might appease Esau (he probably spaced them out as a strategy to make it appear as if there were more animals than there really were) and entice him in accepting his brother.

So Jacob sends the presents to Esau, and he lets his wives, their maids, and all his children and possessions cross the river Jabbok, just outside the land of Canaan. He stays behind that evening—possibly to spend time in prayer before he meets Esau—and by the time the sun comes up, he has experienced one of the most remarkable nights of his life.

WRESTLING AND RECONCILIATION

As night falls and he sits alone by the river, Jacob's thoughts are focused on his coming confrontation with Esau. As Rabbi Telushkin says:

> The night before the encounter with Esau may well have been the most frightening in Jacob's life. Will God keep his promise? Will Esau be propitiated by his gifts? If not, will Jacob's troops be able to successfully fend off Esau's four hundred men? Or will tomorrow be the last day of his and his family's life?

Mentally grappling with these issues, Jacob suddenly finds himself in a physical wrestling match with a stranger that lasts all night long, until the breaking of day. When morning comes, neither man has prevailed, so the stranger touches Jacob on the hip socket, pulling his hip out of joint as they wrestle. The man tells Jacob

"The Struggle of Jacob with the Angel," by Eugene Delacroix. Jewish tradition holds that the angel of Genesis 32 is Michael the Archangel, who is believed to be commander of God's angels. Many Christians, however, believe that Biblical references to the "angel of the Lord" refer to God Himself—specifically, to a pre-incarnate appearance by Jesus Christ.

to let him go, but a fiercely determined Jacob says, "'I will not let you go unless you bless me'" (Genesis 32:26). The man asks Jacob's name, and after Jacob answers, he says, "'Your name shall no longer be called Jacob, but Israel ["he strives with God"], for you have striven with God and with men, and have prevailed'" (Genesis 32:28). The man will not reveal his own name, but blesses Jacob before he leaves. Jacob names the place Peniel ("the face of God"), saying, "'For I have seen God face to face, and yet my life has been delivered'" (Genesis 32:30).

So who is the man with whom Jacob wrestles all night? The name that Jacob gives the site, as well as Hosea's commentary in Hosea 12:3–4 ("in his manhood he [Jacob] strove with God. He strove with the angel and prevailed; he wept and sought his favor.") indicates that the man was not just an angel, but the angel of the Lord, also known as an appearance of God himself.

Jacob's new name—Israel—has great implications for him. It is not unusual in the Bible and in Jewish life for adults to be given new names that mark a crisis and signify a new character or direction, but "no name change . . . has been as significant or peculiar as that of Jacob," says one Jewish scholar. Jacob is no longer just one who deceives or supplants. He is now a man who struggles with and for God. (The Septuagint—a Greek translation of the Hebrew scriptures—translates Genesis 32:28 as "You have been strong with God.") John MacArthur says the name change is "an amazing evaluation of what Jacob had accomplished, i.e., emerging victorious from the struggle. In the record of his life, struggle did dominate with his brother Esau, with his father, with his father-in-law, with his wives and with God at Peniel." From this point on, Jacob and Israel are used interchangeably for the man Jacob and the Jewish nation that descended from him. Jews eventually become known as B'nai Yisra'el, the "children of Israel."

The entire incident shows Jacob that he needs to let go of his own attempts to control his life and surrender to God's desires for him; when he realizes that he truly needs God's blessing, he doggedly persists until he obtains it. The wrestling match is a fitting summary for his entire life.

As a result of that night, Jacob walks with a limp—the sinew of his hip never regains its elasticity. The incident becomes the basis for a dietary restriction for the people of Israel—until at least the time of Moses, they did "not eat the sinew of the thigh that is on the hip socket, because he [the angel] touched the socket of Jacob's hip on the sinew of the thigh" (Genesis 32:32). This law is not found anywhere else in the Old Testament or Mosaic Law, but it is enshrined as a sacred law in the Jewish Talmud. The Qur'an says that all food was lawful to the Israelites (until the Torah was revealed) except for what Israel himself (Jacob) prohibited. Some Muslim teachers believe that Jacob prohibited the eating of the sinews because he suffered from sciatica caused by the angel with whom he wrestled. Others claim that he prohibited camel meat and milk (his favorite food) because he had vowed to give them up if God cured his sciatica.

Reconciliation with Esau

As the sun rises, a reassured Jacob limps off to face his brother. He is reentering the Promised Land at dawn after leaving it the night after he camped at Bethel. He had endured the "long, dark night of exile from the land," as one scholar says, and was coming home. As Esau approaches with his 400 men, Jacob divides his family in a manner that clearly shows his favoritism—he places the maids with their servants in the front, then Leah with her children, and finally, Rachel and Joseph. He walks ahead of them, bowing low to the ground seven times (a common court ritual) until he reaches Esau, still wondering how his brother is going to react. Is Esau about to attack with his 400 men? Or have the presents appeased his wrath?

Genesis 33:4 provides the answer: "But Esau ran to meet him and embraced him and fell on his neck and kissed him, and they wept." Jacob's relief must have been palpable—he knows that his brother no longer hates him. He says to Esau later, "'I have seen your face, which is like seeing the face of God, and you have accepted me'" (Genesis 33:10). Esau does not have murderous rage expressed on his features anymore; he now has an expression of brotherly love and kindness. The scriptures do not say what brought about his change of heart, other than the

Leah, Rachel, and their children watch as Jacob and Esau are reconciled in Canaan. Jewish legend indicates that although Jacob generously gives an expensive gift to his brother as a peace offering, he did not suffer financially. "God 'filled the vacuum without delay,'" writes scholar Louis Ginzberg, "and Jacob was as rich as before."

insinuation that God has worked the change. Perhaps Esau has simply cooled off after so many years, or the change could be a fulfillment of Solomon's wisdom recorded in Proverbs 16:7: "When a man's ways please the Lord, he makes even his enemies to be at peace with him." No more is written of any enmity between the brothers. They live separately but peacefully for the rest of their lives; the only other recorded instance of their being together is when they bury their father Isaac.

That is still several years in the future—for now, Esau is curious about Jacob's family, so Jacob introduces them as "'the children whom God has graciously given your servant'" (Genesis 33:5). He is more and more depending on God and giving him credit for the gracious things that have occurred in his life. Introductions complete, Esau then asks Jacob why he sent such an extravagant gift to him. Jacob tells him he is attempting to find favor in his sight, and Esau responds that he has plenty of his own flocks, so Jacob should keep the gift. Jacob pushes the issue, arguing that Esau should accept the blessing Jacob had brought to him because "'God has dealt graciously with me, and because I have enough'" (Genesis 33:11). The narrative does not explicitly say, but it is possible that Jacob is attempting to make amends for the birthright and blessing he stole from Esau so many years before. He has been blessed, so he wants to return the blessing that rightfully belonged to Esau.

Esau finally agrees to take the animals, and he then urges Jacob to travel home with him. Jacob is leery of doing so, saying that he cannot move quickly because of his children and his nursing flocks and herds. Esau offers to leave some of his people to assist Jacob, but he again declines. The biblical narrative says that Jacob plans to visit Esau where he lives in Seir (also known as Edom, located south of the Promised Land), but the Bible does not record Jacob ever making the trip. Instead, he stops in Succoth, along the Jordan River, where he builds "booths" for his flocks, and then later moves to Shechem in northern Canaan, about 65 miles north of Jerusalem. This was probably around 1908 BCE; the Bible says he came there "safely" (Genesis 33:18), which refers back to the promise God made to Jacob at Bethel so many years before—that he would bring Jacob back safely to the Promised Land.

Strangely, though, Jacob does not return to Bethel to fulfill the vow he had made to God when he left Canaan. He stops in Shechem, only about 20 miles short of Bethel. Scripture does not say why he does not return all the way—perhaps there was better land in Shechem, or Jacob wants better access to the Canaanites he finds there. Whatever the reason, his decision not to fully complete his vow has tragic consequences, as he will soon find out.

Once in Shechem, he buys a piece of land for a hundred pieces of money (exactly what kind of money is unclear), pitches his tents there, and erects an altar to God, which he calls El-Elohe-Israel, meaning "God, the God of Israel." Abraham had built an altar to God in the same spot many years before. Jacob's naming of the altar foreshadows that an entire nation would one day be called Israel, although at the moment, that nation consists mainly of his immediate family.

Jacob also digs a well at Shechem so he will have a permanent water supply. It becomes known as Jacob's Well, and it was still there in New Testament times—the gospels even record Jesus speaking with a woman from Samaria at the well. The scriptures do not say exactly how long Jacob and his family stay at Shechem, but since his sons are young boys when he arrives and grow to be strong young men before he leaves, he probably resides there for about 10 years or so.

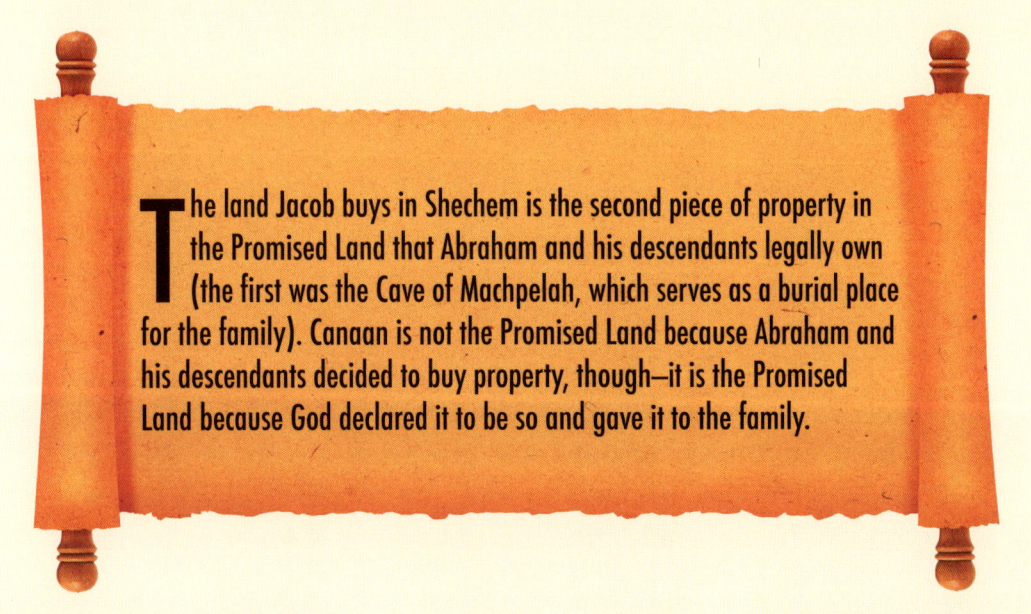

The land Jacob buys in Shechem is the second piece of property in the Promised Land that Abraham and his descendants legally own (the first was the Cave of Machpelah, which serves as a burial place for the family). Canaan is not the Promised Land because Abraham and his descendants decided to buy property, though—it is the Promised Land because God declared it to be so and gave it to the family.

DINAH

The biblical narrative turns next to a difficult episode in the life of Jacob. His daughter Dinah has grown into a woman of marriageable age as the family lives in Shechem. One day, she ventures out to see the women of the land, most likely just to see how they live and compare it to her own life. She has no idea that her day trip will have disastrous consequences.

As she is out, Shechem, the son of Hamor (his name is the same as the name of the city) sees her and desires to have her, so he takes her by force and rapes her. Afterward, his "soul was drawn to Dinah" (Genesis 34:3), and he loves her and asks his father to get her for him as a wife.

Jacob hears of the incident but wants to wait to respond until he can hold council with his sons, who are out in the fields; he may also have felt too weak for a confrontation without them. Hamor arrives to speak with Jacob as Jacob's sons come in from the fields. As would be expected, they "were indignant and very angry, because he [Shechem] had done an outrageous thing in Israel by lying with Jacob's daughter" (Genesis 34:7). Hamor informs the family that his son longs to marry Dinah, and he pleads his case, saying:

> "Make marriages with us. Give your daughters to us, and take our daughters for yourselves. You shall dwell with us, and the land shall be open to you. Dwell and trade in it, and get property in it."
> (Genesis 34:8–10)

Shechem also tries to convince them to agree to the marriage, saying, "'Let me find favor in your eyes, and whatever you say to me I will give. Ask me for as great a bride price and gift as you will, and I will give whatever you say to me. Only give me the young woman to be my wife'" (Genesis 34:11–12). Notably absent from their appeals is any sort of apology or even acknowledgement of Shechem's rape of Dinah. They also seem to be negotiating as if everything is normal, but they are still holding Dinah captive back in Shechem's house.

Apparently the two men think their words will be enough to convince Jacob and his sons to overlook the evil that Shechem has done. They "painted a picture of harmonious integration" with Israel, one scholar says, but later told the men of their own city that if the deal went through, all of Jacob's livestock, property and animals would become theirs. Not only is it a bad proposal, but it runs directly counter to God's desire that the people of Israel not inter-

The Rape of Dinah, daughter of Jacob and Leah. The clothing and architecture shown in this 1531 painting clearly reflect trends of the European Renaissance.

marry with foreigners from Canaan. Deuteronomy 7:3–6 spells out God's principle for marriage that was in effect even before it was written down: "You shall not intermarry with them, giving your daughters to their sons or taking their daughters for your sons, for they would turn away your sons from following me, to serve other gods . . . for you are a people holy to the Lord your God. The Lord your God has chosen you to be a people for his treasured possession, out of all the peoples who are on the face of the earth."

Jacob's sons answer Shechem and his father deceitfully (the old family trait is coming out again), telling them that they cannot give their sister to a man who is uncircumcised—that would be disgraceful to them, as circumcision was a sign of God's covenant with his people. They strike a bargain with Shechem: If all the men of the city will be circumcised (a painful procedure that will also be an appropriate punishment for the crime that has been committed), then they will begin intermarrying among their two peoples.

Shechem and Hamor quickly agree, and because of their honored position in the city, they convince all the men to join them. On the third day after the procedure, when the men are still recovering, Jacob's sons put the rest of their plan into shocking action. In a violent reprisal, Simeon and Levi (who says in his apocryphal testament that he is about 20 years old) take their swords and kill all the males of the city while they cannot defend themselves. They kill Shechem and Hamor and rescue Dinah out of captivity in Shechem's house. The rest of the sons of Israel then join Simeon and Levi in plundering the city and taking flocks, herds, donkeys, women, and children, and all of the wealth they can find.

Jacob is not happy with what his sons have done. He says to Simeon and Levi, "'You have brought trouble on me by making me stink to the inhabitants of the land, the Canaanites and the Perizzites. My numbers are few, and if they gather themselves against me and attack me, I shall be destroyed, both I and my household'" (Genesis 34:30). He does not seem concerned so much about the morality of what they did as the political and economic implications their actions will engender. Their response is filled with the belief that their cause and actions were just: "'Should he treat our sister like a prostitute?'" (Genesis 34:31).

At the end of Jacob's life, he lets his sons know his true disapproval of their actions—as he is blessing all of his sons, he says this about Simeon and Levi:

> "Simeon and Levi are brothers; weapons of violence are their swords. Let my soul come not into their council; O my glory, be not joined to their company. For in their anger they killed men, and in their willfulness they hamstrung oxen. Cursed be their anger, for it is fierce, and their wrath, for it is cruel! I will divide them in Jacob and scatter them in Israel." (Genesis 49:5–7)

The dynamic of the family is changing. Jacob is becoming passive, letting his sons do as they wish, even when

Consequences of Their Actions

Simeon and Levi do suffer consequences as a result of their hot-headed and cruel response to the men of Shechem. Simeon eventually becomes the smallest of the 12 tribes, shares territory with the tribe of Judah, and is left out of the blessing Moses bestows on all of the other tribes just before he dies. As Jacob prophesied, the tribe of Levi is scattered throughout Israel without its own designated territory—the members of the tribe serve as priests for the nation.

their actions are beyond the pale. As MacArthur says, "A massacre of all males and the wholesale plunder of the city went way beyond the reasonable, wise, and justly deserved punishment of one man; this was a considerably more excessive vengeance than the Mosaic Law would later legislate." The law later requires a man who has raped a virgin to pay the girl's father a fine and then marry her with no possibility of divorce. Jacob's sons do far more, but they are also angry because their father has no response to an incident that requires a reaction. Jacob's inability to control his sons will lead to even greater trouble later when they turn on Joseph. In fact, his failure to protect Dinah, the daughter of Leah, could also be part of the motivation for the plot that the sons of Leah hatch against Joseph, who is Jacob's beloved son by Rachel.

In the next verses, Jacob and his family are preparing to move to Bethel, as God has commanded them. Jacob probably should have settled in Bethel when he first returned to Canaan—it is the spot where 30 years before he vowed to follow God, while God promised to bring him back safely to his father's land. Upon Jacob's return, though, he stopped short of Bethel. Now, at least 10 years later, he does not have much of a choice—he has to depart Shechem because of the violence his sons have committed. As William Blaikie says, "He could no longer live in a place where, apart from other considerations, the law of blood revenge must claim him and his family as victims. More than that, his reputation as a neighbor was ruined, and the credit of his religion was shattered."

RACHEL'S DEATH AND JOSEPH'S LIFE

As the family prepares to leave for Bethel, where Jacob will fulfill his vow to the God of his fathers, it is time for them to remove all traces of any sort of idol worship. "'Put away the foreign gods that are among you and purify yourselves and change your garments,'" Jacob tells his family. "'Then let us arise and go up to Bethel, so that I may make there an altar to the God who answers me in the day of my distress and has been with me wherever I have gone'" (Genesis 35:2–3). This purification is in contrast to the defilement at Shechem. His family, most likely numb from shock at what the brothers did and fearful of reprisal, quickly comply with his instructions. They give Jacob all the foreign gods they have (this would include the household idols Rachel stole from her father), along with rings from their ears (often made in the shape of gods and goddesses). Jacob buries them under a terebinth tree near Shechem, ridding himself and his family of their destructive influence. Jacob's language here —"Put away the foreign gods that are among you" (Genesis 35:2) — is echoed later by reformers in Israel and shows, as the Anchor Bible Dictionary says, that "the sly loner . . . has become the zealous religious leader of a people."

COVENANT RENEWED

As they travel south to Bethel, God protects the family from retaliation by the peoples of the land: "A terror from God fell upon the cities that were around them, so that they did not pursue the sons of Jacob" (Genesis 35:5). When the large group reaches its destination, Jacob builds another altar and renames the place El-bethel ("the God of Bethel"), thus reaffirming his commitment to God and fulfilling the promise he had made in Genesis 28:20–22 as he set out for Haran about 30 years before: "'If God will be with me and will keep me in this way that I go, and will give me bread to eat and clothing to wear, so that I come again to my father's house in peace, then the Lord shall be my God, and this stone, which I have set up for a pillar, shall be God's house.'" God then appears to him and again tells Jacob that he will be called Israel. He also repeats his promise to give the land around him to his offspring, and he encourages Jacob to be fruitful and multiply, for nations would come from him, and "'kings shall come forth from your own body'" (Genesis 35:11). God has not used this language about kings since he covenanted with Abraham; the promise hints at the future royalty to come, most notably David and Jesus Christ. When God finishes speaking with him, Jacob sets up another stone pillar and pours out both a drink offering and oil upon it, a common way to seal a covenant.

RACHEL'S DEATH

Apparently there is not sufficient pastureland around Bethel for Jacob's large flocks and herds, so he heads south, toward Bethlehem. The reader does not yet know that Rachel is pregnant again, but while on the journey, she goes into a difficult labor that will result in her death. Just as her labor reaches its hardest point, her midwife tells her she has given birth to another son. As she is dying, she calls his name Ben-oni ("son of my sorrow"), but Jacob calls him Benjamin ("son of my right hand"). The scriptures do not say anything of Jacob's reaction, but he must be devastated at the death of his beloved Rachel. This is the woman he loved, the one he had worked 14

Jacob and his children mourn the death of Rachel, who died while giving birth to a son, Benjamin.

84 *Jacob*

Pilgrims visit the shrine at Rachel's tomb near Bethlehem, circa 1898. The scriptures do not say why Jacob does not bury Rachel in the family tomb (the Cave of Machpelah) only 12 miles south, but it is most likely because Rachel is not his first wife and cannot therefore be accorded that privilege.

years for the privilege of marrying. Now that she is gone, his great love for her will transfer to her two sons, Joseph and Benjamin, which plays no small part in the favoritism that will soon lead to enormous problems.

Jacob buries Rachel about a mile north of Bethlehem and sets up a pillar over her tomb that is still there when Moses later writes Genesis. Today there is a small, square building in a lonely spot, with a dome on top that has the name of Rachel's tomb written on it. It is not the pillar built by Jacob, but it does likely mark the spot where she was buried.

REUBEN'S SIN

After Rachel's death, Jacob pitches his tents for a while near a watchtower close to Bethlehem. He needs some time to think, to process all that has happened recently and to decide his next move. While they dwell there, the Bible says that Reuben went and lay with Bilhah, his father's concubine. Such a deed in those times was not just a sexual act, but was generally seen as the son staking his claim to his father's role and leadership position. (Absalom later does the same thing to his father David.) Genesis 35:22 simply says that Jacob heard of it. That is all. He does not respond and he does not rebuke or punish Reuben. He has shifted into passive mode, willing to let his sons do whatever they feel like. There are consequences for Reuben down the road, though—because of his sin, Jacob eventually strips away the title and privilege of firstborn son. In his deathbed blessing of his sons, he tells Reuben: "'Reuben, you are my firstborn, my might, and the firstfruits of my strength, preeminent in dignity and preeminent in power. Unstable as water, you shall not have preeminence, because you went up to your father's bed; then you defiled it—he went up to my couch!'" (Genesis 49:3–4)

THE DEATH OF ISAAC

Jacob eventually makes his way to Hebron (south of Bethlehem), where his father Isaac still lives. There is no mention of Rebekah—she has presumably died much earlier. The scriptures say nothing of the details of Isaac and Jacob's reunion, only that Jacob does get to see him before he dies at 180 years old. Esau is there as well, and he and Jacob bury Isaac together, in the tomb of his fathers at the Cave of Machpelah, around 1885 BCE Jacob and Esau seem to conclude this transaction in peace, and they go their separate ways, "content to follow the lines marked out for them," as one scholar describes. In fact, they seem to have agreed that Esau would go back to the land of

Edom (out of the land of Canaan), because they both have vast amounts of family, possessions, goods, and livestock. As Genesis 36:7 says, "Their possessions were too great for them to dwell together. The land of their sojournings could not support them because of their livestock."

This is a fitting conclusion to their relationship—God had promised that Abraham's descendants through Jacob would inherit the land, so it is appropriate that he remain in Canaan while Esau moves on. The scriptures do not say if Esau ever accepts God's covenant relationship with his brother, but in any case, he makes no more trouble about it.

Jacob settles near Hebron to tend to his vast flocks and herds, finally secure in the knowledge that he is dwelling in the land God had promised him, the land of his father's sojournings. According to Josephus, an early Jewish historian: "It happened that Jacob came to so great happiness as rarely any other person had arrived at. He was richer than the rest of the inhabitants of that country. . . . And God exercised such a providence over him, and such a care of his happiness, as to bring him the greatest blessings, even out of what appeared to be the most sorrowful condition." His flocks and herds by this point must have been enormous, given that all of his sons' full-time jobs involved managing the animals and household. And that fact means that Jacob was enormously wealthy for the time. Exchangeable money has not fully developed yet, so animals are just as valuable to their owners as their equivalent value in silver or gold would be. As *The Anchor Bible Dictionary* puts it, "Abraham and the other patriarchs counted their wealth in numbers of sheep, goats, and cattle . . . throughout the period of the patriarchs and into the time of the kings of Israel and Judah the primary means of commerce and trade was barter. Money could be metallic and weighed . . . or it could be in kind."

This colored 19th-century postcard shows Hebron, the ancient city where Jacob and his son settled in Canaan. Hebron is located about 20 miles (32 km) southwest of Jerusalem, and situated in a fertile, well-watered valley. The city is mentioned 87 times in the Old Testament.

FAVORED SON

The biblical narrative shifts perspective at this point, moving primarily from Jacob's experience to focus on the life of Joseph, Jacob's 11th son, but the first by his wife Rachel and therefore Jacob's favorite. This favoritism—and Jacob's increasing lack of control over his sons—is the source of much of the conflict that follows. Joseph's brothers, who will one day be the heads of the tribes of Israel, are a restless, jealous, conflicted lot. They are not oblivious—it is easy for them to tell that Jacob loved Joseph's mother more than he loved their mothers, and so by extension he loves Joseph more than them.

In Genesis 37:1–4, Joseph appears for the first time since his birth. He is 17 years old and working as a shepherd for his father:

> Jacob lived in the land of his father's sojournings, in the land of Canaan. These are the generations of Jacob. Joseph, being seventeen years old, was pasturing the flock with his brothers. He was a boy with the sons of Bilhah and Zilpah, his father's wives. And Joseph brought a bad report of them to their father. Now Israel loved Joseph more than any other of his sons, because he was the son of his old age. And he made him a robe of many colors. But when his brothers saw that their father loved him more than all his brothers, they hated him and could not speak peacefully to him.

Even though Reuben is Jacob's firstborn son, the passage skips straight to Joseph when it begins describing Jacob's descendants. This is a mark of Joseph's favored status, as well as an indication of the truth—in the end, Joseph becomes more prominent than any of his brothers. In addition to Jacob's love for Rachel, several other factors play into his favoritism of Joseph. Josephus writes that Jacob loves him because of the "beauty of his body and the virtues of his mind, for he excelled the rest in prudence." A traditional Jewish legend suggests that Joseph "resembled his father most closely in appearance," and that the entire course of his life echoes that of Jacob's. Legend also says that Joseph becomes so learned by the age of 17 that he could teach even his older brothers. According to another scholar, Joseph's gifts go a long ways toward explaining Jacob's affections: "It was not unnatural for Jacob to have a special affection for Joseph . . . because that interesting mixture of grace and talent which afterwards shone out in him so remarkably, and which was such a contrast to the coarseness of his brothers, had won his heart and had knit the souls of father and son into a wonderful unity."

But Joseph is not marked only by Jacob's love—his brothers' hatred and anger toward him is palpable. Josephus says that the "affection of his [Joseph's] father excited the envy and the hatred of his brethren." Nothing makes that more clear than the coat of many colors that Jacob gives Joseph. It is an elaborate, hand-sewn garment of great distinction that is probably long-sleeved and full-length—not something a hardworking shepherd would typically wear while working in the fields and herding flocks each day. This kind of garment confers favor and elevated status upon the one who wears it; a patriarch would usually give it to the son he intends one day to lead the household. By presenting the coat to Joseph and thereby raising the younger brother above his elders, Jacob is breaking with the patrilineal tradition of passing titles, privileges and inheritances to the firstborn son. Joseph's brothers know this, and so they hate the coat and all that it represents. They cannot even speak peacefully to Joseph, so great is their hatred for him and his relationship with their father. Simeon says in his apocryphal testament: "For in the time of my youth I was jealous in many things of Joseph, because my father loved him beyond all. And I set my mind against him to destroy him because the prince of deceit sent forth the spirit of jealousy and blinded my mind, so that I regarded him not as a brother, nor did I spare even Jacob my father" (Testament of Simeon 1:7–8).

According to the Qur'an, when the brothers consider how important Joseph is to their father, they begin to make plans to do away with him: "Surely, Joseph and his brother [Benjamin] are dearer to our father than ourselves, though we are many. Truly, our father is much mistaken. Let us slay Joseph, or cast him away in some far-off land, so that we may have no rivals in our father's love, and after that be honourable men" (Penguin Books, Translated with notes by N.J. Dawood, 1993, Qur'an 12:8–9,).

Joseph does not help matters any when he tells his brothers of two dreams which imply that they (and his father and mother) will bow down to Joseph. After hearing the second dream, his brothers ridicule him, and Jacob says, "'What is this dream that you have dreamed? Shall I and your mother and your brothers indeed come to bow ourselves to the ground before you?'" (Genesis 37:10). His father keeps the dream in mind—a hint, perhaps, that he thinks some truth might come of it, as indeed it does many years later. Josephus says that "Jacob was pleased with the dream: for, considering the prediction in his mind, and shrewdly and wisely guessing at its meaning, he rejoiced at the great things thereby signified, because it declared the future happiness of his son; and that, by the blessing of God, the time would come when he should be honored."

Sometime after Joseph's dreams, Jacob sends the brothers to pasture his flock near Shechem (the same city where Dinah had been raped). Joseph does not go with them, but Jacob later asks him to check on the men and bring back word of their situation. He thinks it will be a short trip for Joseph; in reality, he will not see his son again for more than 20 years.

JOSEPH SOLD INTO SLAVERY

Joseph's brothers see him approaching their camp from a distance and decide their opportunity to be rid of him has come. They plan with obvious malice and intent to kill him and throw him in a pit: "We will say that a fierce animal has devoured him, and we will see what will become of his dreams" (Genesis 37:20). Reuben proposes throwing him in the pit first, rather than killing him, which they do. While he is then away, his brothers hit upon a solution for getting rid of Joseph without killing him. Their campsite is on the path of an ancient trade route, so they sell Joseph to a band of slave traders traveling to Egypt. When Reuben returns and finds Joseph gone, he tears his clothes in grief and fear because he knows his father will hold him responsible for Joseph's disappearance—Reuben, after all, is still the firstborn. To explain Joseph's absence to their father, the brothers slaughter a goat and dip Joseph's robe in the blood, creating the impression that he has been devoured by a wild animal.

They send the robe back to Jacob, feigning innocence as they ask him to identify whether or not it is Joseph's. Even with Joseph now gone, they are still calculating and cruel, tricking their father into thinking his beloved son has been brutally killed. For his part, Jacob is grief-struck at Joseph's loss: "Then Jacob tore his garments and put sackcloth on his loins and mourned his son many days. All

Weighed, Not Counted

Before the Hebrew people first used coins (sometime around the fifth century BCE), precious metals such as gold and silver were weighed for their value rather than counted out as money. Some units of weight later became the name of a coin. Biblical currency can be compared with today's monetary values, but the buying power of money has changed so much that exact comparisons are not always possible.

The word *shekel* is actually the Hebrew word for weight. In the ancient Jewish system, a common shekel weighed about 0.4 ounces (or about 11.5 grams). Joseph's brothers sold him for 20 silver shekels, the average price of a slave at the time. To put it into perspective, one silver shekel was equal to four days' wages for a common laborer.

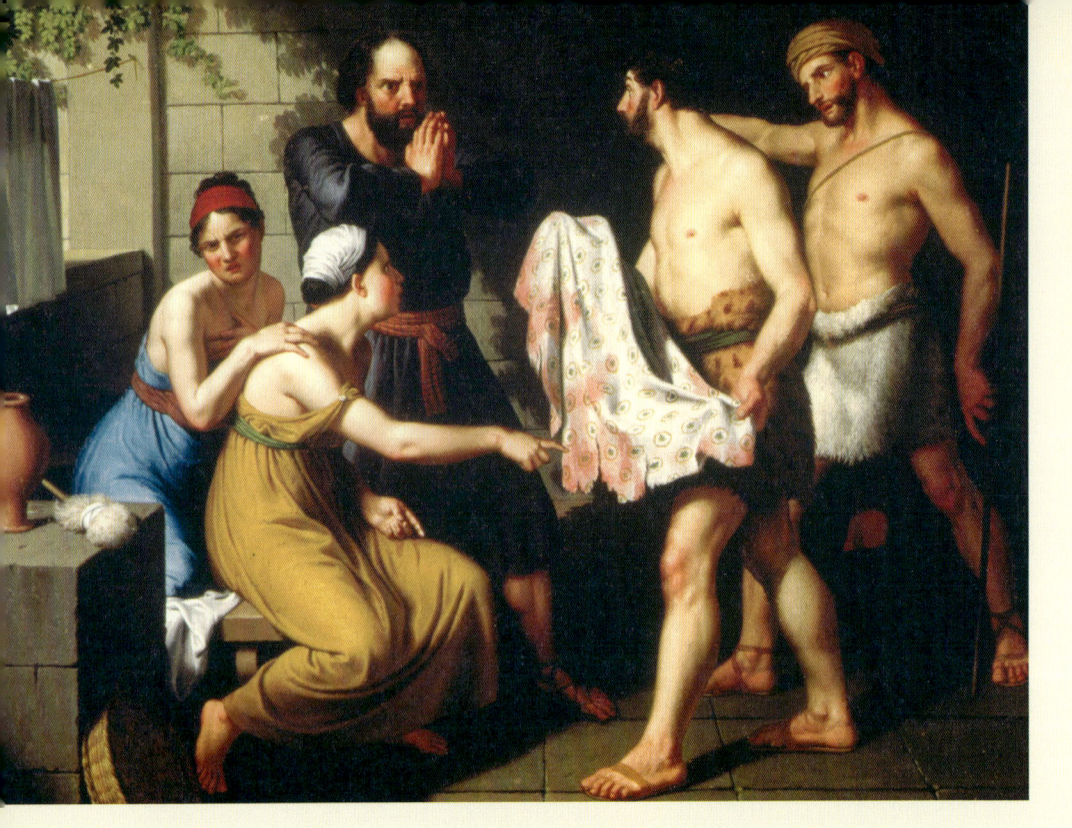

A folktale describes what happened when Joseph's brothers presented the bloodstained coat to their father: "Jacob recognized Joseph's coat, and, overwhelmed by grief, he fell prostrate, and long lay on the ground motionless, like a stone. Then he arose, and set up a loud cry, and wept, saying, 'It is my son's coat.'"

his sons and all his daughters rose up to comfort him, but he refused to be comforted and said, 'No, I shall go down to Sheol [the place of the dead] to my son, mourning.' Thus his father wept for him" (Genesis 37:34–35). His sons try to comfort him, but they fail to offer the one thing that will bring true relief to Jacob's heart—the truth. In an unexpected twist of providence, Jacob is suffering because his sons have perpetrated the same sort of deceit on him that he used on his own father many years before, when he defrauded his brother of his rightful blessing. He even used the same two elements as his sons—a slaughtered goat and a garment. Unlike his own deceit, though, it will be more than two decades before he learns the truth about what really happened to Joseph.

9

JOSEPH IN EGYPT

While Jacob is mourning the loss of his beloved son, Joseph is working his way to the top in Egypt. The slave traders sell him to Potiphar, the captain of the guard and an officer of Pharaoh, the king of Egypt. He proves himself to be so talented and trustworthy as Potiphar's slave that Potiphar promotes him to run his entire estate. The only thing Potiphar concerns himself with is the food he eats—everything else is under Joseph's care. Joseph does well there and in future environments because he has a unique ability to assess the situation he is in and determine the best course of action. And he has something no one else in Egypt does: the God of his fathers is with him. Five times in the first five verses of Genesis 39, the Bible refers to the Lord's presence or blessing on Joseph and all his activities.

Joseph is put to a severe test when Potiphar's wife attempts to seduce him. Day after day she pursues him, and he firmly refuses, telling her he cannot commit this sin against God and man. One day, she finally tries to pull him into bed when no one else is around, but he flees, leaving his robe in her hands. She accuses him of trying to rape her, and as a result, Potiphar throws Joseph in prison for a crime he did not commit.

Again, Joseph excels in a new environment. The keeper of the prison puts him in charge of running the jail, and while there, he meets Pharaoh's chief cupbearer and baker, both of whom have dreams they ask Joseph to interpret. He does so correctly, but when the chief cupbearer is restored to his position, he forgets that Joseph asked him to inform Pharaoh of Joseph's predicament. For two more long years, Joseph languishes in jail, but he never departs from his belief in God. He has been thrown into a pit, sold into slavery, falsely accused, imprisoned, and now completely forgotten. But he never speaks ill of God, and he continues to believe that God is working for a good greater than he can see in his current situation. Several years later, he expresses this overarching belief when he says to his brothers in Genesis 50:20 that "'you meant it for evil, but God meant it for good.'"

Joseph Promoted

After two years, Pharaoh has a pair of dreams that neither he nor his wise men can interpret. The chief cupbearer finally remembers his experience with Joseph, so Pharaoh sends for him. Joseph, giving the credit to God, correctly interprets the dreams to mean that Egypt is facing seven good years of plenty followed by seven difficult years of famine. Pharaoh is so impressed by the wisdom that God has given Joseph that he immediately promotes him—at the age of 30—to second in command of the entire country, answerable only to Pharaoh himself. Jacob's son, a lowly

Pharaoh, surrounded by advisers and seated on an opulent throne, listens to Joseph interpret his dreams.

Hebrew slave, has risen to command Egypt, one of the mightiest nations on earth.

Pharaoh bestows on Joseph power and riches beyond anything he could have imagined while in his jail cell. He gives him gold, silver, land, a new wardrobe, a palace, slaves, and jewels. Joseph also has Pharaoh's signet ring, which grants him unlimited access and power to conduct all needful transactions and affairs of state on behalf of Pharaoh. Joseph marries an Egyptian woman named Asenath, and they have two sons together: Ephraim and Manasseh.

As a ruler, Joseph takes the skills he had learned as a manager of flocks, households, and prisons and applies them on a much larger scale to an entire country. His most immediate challenge is preparing the country for the coming famine; his plan is to store as much food as possible dur-

Joseph exercises his duties as Pharaoh's viceroy. He is attended by a scribe, who records Joseph's decrees on papyrus scrolls.

ing the seven years of plenty. To accomplish this, he travels frequently through the entire land of Egypt (about the size of Texas and New Mexico together), providing direction for the gathering and storage of one-fifth of all the grain. He builds huge granaries in every city so that area farmers can easily store the grain that comes from surrounding fields.

FAMINE COMES

As Joseph had predicted, the seven years of plenty come to an end, and the famine begins in earnest throughout Egypt and neighboring countries, including Canaan, where Jacob still lives with his family. Famine was no ordinary occurrence in that part of the world—it was a rare event caused by a lack of rain in the upper regions of the Nile River. The dearth of water meant that crops simply could not grow—they would wither and shrivel in the hardpan soil that had been baked dry by the blazing sun.

Historians tell of a similar kind of famine that devastated Egypt in the 12th century CE. Eyewitnesses recount terrible details: "The poor ate carrion, corpses and dogs . . . as for the number of the poor who perished from hunger and exhaustion, God alone knows what it was . . . A traveler often passed through a large village without seeing a single inhabitant. . . . The road between Syria and Egypt [which would have passed through or near Canaan] was like a vast field sown with human bodies."

Joseph's foresight and planning save Egypt and surrounding countries from this kind of disaster, as the Bible records:

> There was famine in all lands, but in all the land of Egypt there was bread. When all the land of Egypt was famished, the people cried to Pharaoh for bread. Pharaoh said to all the Egyptians, "Go to Joseph. What he says to you, do." So when the famine had spread over all the land, Joseph opened all the storehouses and sold to the Egyptians, for the famine was severe in the land of Egypt. Moreover, all the earth came to Egypt to Joseph to buy grain, because the famine was severe over all the earth. (Genesis 41:54–57)

As word spreads that Egypt has grain available, citizens from other countries begin to trickle into Egypt, looking for the man Joseph, who is responsible for handing out grain to his own countrymen and strangers alike. The historian Josephus attributes Joseph's generosity to his sense of the brotherhood of man: "Nor did he open this market of corn for the people of that country only, but strangers had liberty to buy also; Joseph being willing that all men, who are naturally akin to one another, should have assistance from those that lived in happiness."

JACOB REENTERS THE PICTURE

It has been 22 years since Joseph has heard anything about his family. (Joseph was 17 when he was sold into slavery and 30 when he stood before Pharaoh. He then governed the land during seven years of plenty, and, as is revealed later, through the first two years of famine before his brothers came to Egypt.) Joseph must be wondering what his brothers are like now, how many nieces and nephews he has, and if his father is even still alive. His responsibility for selling grain gives him a good vantage point to watch for his family members—Jewish legend says he even requires all those who buy grain to give their names so that he might locate his family if they show up. The Bible, the Qur'an, and Jewish history say nothing about Joseph attempting to locate his family once he comes to power in Egypt. It seems unlikely that he would not have wanted to at least contact his father, but there is no definite reason why he did not. Perhaps the business of running a country and preparing for a great famine simply took all of his time.

In any case, Jacob and his family have enough stored food to last through the first two years of the famine. To have that many provisions laid up—enough for his entire household, including his children, their families, and servants—means that Jacob planned well and was a man of substantial means. Most sojourning shepherds probably did not have that much in reserve, but God's blessing and Jacob's astute management had brought him an abundance of animals and goods. Now, though, with two years of famine behind them and no end in sight, the food is almost gone. Jacob's sons appear paralyzed about what to do, but Jacob has heard of the abundance in Egypt, so he sends them to buy food for the entire clan, saying, "'Go down and buy grain for us there, that we may live and not die'"

(Genesis 42:2). He does not send his youngest son, Benjamin (Joseph's full brother, who by this time is at least in his 20s), on the trip; he fears that harm could just as easily befall Benjamin, as it had Joseph so many years before.

THE BROTHERS IN EGYPT

The same 10 brothers—Reuben, Simeon, Levi, Judah, Dan, Naphtali, Gad, Asher, Issachar, and Zebulun—who sold Joseph into slavery set off for the land of Egypt, intent on buying grain for their family. When they arrive, they "bowed themselves before him [Joseph] with their faces to the ground . . . and Joseph recognized his brothers, but they did not recognize him. And Joseph remembered the dreams that he had dreamed of them" (Genesis 42:7–9). This is a transcendent moment for Joseph. His brothers, who had sold him as if he were mere property 20 years before, are bowing in front of him, just as his dreams had foretold.

There is no reason Jacob's sons should recognize their younger brother. He is obviously a high-ranking Egyptian official, wearing Egyptian garments and fluent in the Egyptian tongue. For his part, Joseph speaks harshly to them and repeatedly accuses them of being spies, possibly to buy some time to decide the best course of action. In response to Joseph's accusations, his brothers tell him they are not spies, but are all the sons (along with two others) of

> Joseph's accusation of spying would have caused his brothers real fear—they knew that Egypt was most vulnerable to invasion from the northern side of the country (where Canaan was located), so Egyptian officials were always on the lookout for spies from that area.

one man. Of the two sons who did not make the trip, they tell Joseph that the youngest was with their father, and "'one is no more'" (Genesis 42:13). Joseph tells them the only way to prove their truthfulness is to bring their youngest brother to Egypt, and he tosses them in jail for three days while everyone thinks things over. He still has not revealed himself to his brothers—he may be concealing his identity

When Was Joseph in Egypt?

Establishing dates for Joseph's time in Egypt is difficult, if not impossible. Some scholars place Joseph in Egypt during the reign of the Hyksos (ca. 1730 to 1570 BCE). A Semitic tribe from Canaan known as the "shepherd kings," the Hyksos were racially and culturally related to the Hebrews and would presumably have been friendly with them. Some evidence—including burial sites, pottery, and building styles—links the Hyksos period to the time the Israelites spent in Egypt. A Semitic king in power would help explain Joseph's ascendance and Pharaoh's immediate acceptance of Joseph's family (who were shepherds) when they came to Egypt.

Other scholars date Joseph's time in Egypt to the 12th dynasty (ca. 1991–1786 BCE), which was part of the Middle Kingdom period of Egyptian history. They argue that the cultural clues from the biblical account point to Egyptian, not Semitic, rulers. For example, the names in the Joseph narrative are Egyptian (also, it is difficult to imagine why a Hyksos pharaoh would give Joseph an Egyptian name, as occurs in Genesis 41:45). Furthermore, Joseph shaves before his audience with Pharaoh (Genesis 41:14), but a Hyksos king would not have been offended by a beard. Finally, when Joseph's brothers first come to Egypt, they openly discuss their dilemma in front of him (not realizing who he is); if they thought he was a Hyksos ruler, they would have known he did not need an interpreter to understand their confidential conversation.

to glean more information about his father and Benjamin.

He wants to see his younger brother very much, so he tells the 10 brothers they may travel home and return with Benjamin if they leave one of their number behind as surety for their return. The brothers agree to the plan, but their guilt over their treatment of Joseph 22 years before has begun working overtime as a result of their trip to Egypt—the same journey Joseph would have taken. "They said to one another, 'In truth, we are guilty concerning our brother, in that we saw the distress of his soul, when he begged us and we did not listen. That is why this distress has come upon us'" (Genesis 42:21). Joseph hears their discussion and is overcome with emotion. He then orders his servants to fill the brothers' grain bags and give them provisions for the trip home; without the brothers' knowledge, he also directs that the money they paid for the grain should be returned to them in their bags. They leave Simeon behind with Joseph and travel back to Canaan.

DEBATING AT HOME

Once home, the nine brothers relate their story to their father, Jacob. As they unload their sacks of grain, they discover that their money has been returned. Instead of rejoicing at their good fortune, though, they are all afraid, especially Jacob, who has developed a negative outlook over the last 20 years. "'You have bereaved me of my children,'" he says. "'Joseph is no more, and Simeon is no more, and now you would take Benjamin. All this has come against me'" (Genesis 42:36). Even though Benjamin is grown, Jacob is determined not to send him to Egypt for fear that he will lose his only other son by Rachel. Reuben offers the lives of his two sons to his father as insurance against Benjamin's life, but Jacob will have none of it. "'My son shall not go down with you, for his brother is dead and he is the only one left. If harm should happen to him on the journey that you are to make, you would bring down my gray hairs with sorrow to Sheol'" (Genesis 42:38).

The problem with his line of thinking is that the famine continues just as severely as before, and the grain the brothers bought in Egypt eventually begins to run out. Jacob, still in denial, tells them to return to Egypt and buy more grain, but he makes no mention of taking Benjamin. Judah reminds him of Joseph's demands: "'The man solemnly warned us, saying, "You shall not see my face unless your brother is with you." If you will send our brother with us, we will go down and buy you food. But if you will not send him, we will not go down, for the man said to us, "You shall not see my face unless your brother is with you."'" (Genesis 43:3–5)

Jacob still refuses, until Judah finally makes an appeal that breaks through his defenses:

> "Send the boy with me, and we will arise and go, that we may live and not die, both we and also our little ones. I will be a pledge of his safety. From my hand you shall require him. If I do not bring him back to you and set him before you, then let me bear the blame forever." (Genesis 43:8–9)

In his argument, Judah points out one inescapable conclusion—if they do not obtain food from Egypt, they and their families will die. The only way to get the food is to take Benjamin with them. It is that simple.

Jacob finally realizes that "it must be so" and bids the brothers carry a present to the Egyptian lord, including "a little balm and a little honey, gum, myrrh, pistachio nuts, and almonds" (Genesis 43:11). These gifts—some of which are still given today—are a significant gesture because Jacob probably has very little food left. But gifts

This map shows the region through which Jacob's sons would have traveled to reach Egypt. Joseph would have ruled the country from the capital at Memphis, on the Nile River.

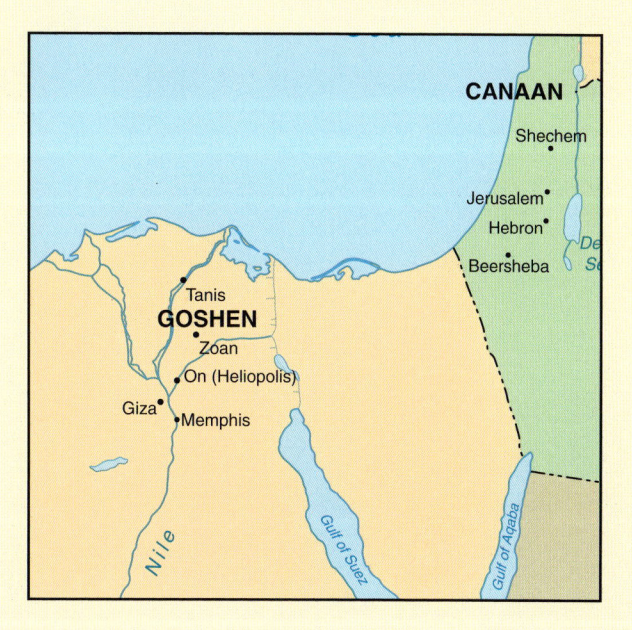

had helped Jacob defuse a difficult situation with his brother Esau, and he is hoping they will work again. He also has his sons take double the usual amount of money with them so they can return what they found in their sacks the first time. In his parting speech, he trusts that God will bless the endeavor, but he also sounds a note of resignation: "'May God Almighty grant you mercy before the man, and may he send back your other brother and Benjamin. And as for me, if I am bereaved of my children, I am bereaved'" (Genesis 43:14).

In his later years, Jacob seems to have forgotten the promises God had made to watch over Jacob and his descendants. He has descended into a spiral of self-pity and depression, but he still recognizes God's power and he will soon be reminded of God's goodness in an unforgettable reunion with a son he thinks is dead.

10

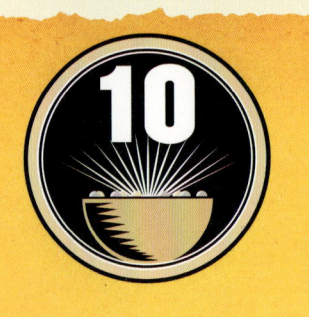

A New Home

When the brothers return to Egypt, they present their father's gift to Joseph. When he recognizes his brother Benjamin, whom he has not seen in more than 20 years, he feels compassion begin to overwhelm him, but he gains control of himself and orders a meal served. The Hebrew brothers are invited to eat at their own table in front of Joseph (Egyptians would not eat at the same table as Hebrews). When they come to sit down, they look at one another in amazement—Joseph has seated all eleven brothers in correct age order, from Reuben down to Benjamin. The meal goes well from both perspectives: "And the brothers drank and were merry with him" (Genesis 43:34).

Joseph senses that his brothers are changed men, but he wants one more piece of proof before he reveals his identity to them. In Jewish tradition, the classic test of repentance is to place people in exactly the same situation that led to their original

A New Home 105

wrongdoing to discover if their actions will be any different after their supposed repentance. To this end, as the brothers prepare to leave the next morning, Joseph commands his steward not only to fill the men's sacks with grain, but once again to return their money and to put his royal silver cup in the mouth of Benjamin's sack. After the brothers leave, Joseph sends his steward to catch up with them, search their sacks, and accuse them of stealing the cup.

When the steward finds the cup in Benjamin's sack, his older brothers tear their clothes in grief and anguish—their father's worst fear of Benjamin not returning is coming true. They return to Joseph's house, where Judah tells him that "'God has found out the guilt of your servants'"

Joseph's cup is found in Benjamin's sack of grain—a test by the vizier to determine whether or not his brothers have truly changed.

(Genesis 44:16). He is referring not just to the silver cup, but to their treatment of Joseph 20 years before. Judah tells Joseph that all the brothers will be his servants, but Joseph replies that it is only necessary for Benjamin to remain—the rest are free to return to their father.

This sets up one of the most dramatic and moving scenes in the Old Testament. Desperate at the thought of his father's grief if Benjamin does not return home, Judah sacrificially pleads with Joseph to let Benjamin return home, using their father Jacob as the main motivation:

> "Oh, my lord, please let your servant speak a word in my lord's ears, and let not your anger burn against your servant, for you are like Pharaoh himself. . . .
>
> "Now therefore, as [my father Jacob's] life is bound up in the boy's life, as soon as he sees that the boy is not with us, he will die, and your servants will bring down the gray hairs of your servant our father with sorrow to Sheol. For your servant became a pledge of safety for the boy to my father, saying, 'If I do not bring him back to you, then I shall bear the blame before my father all my life.' Now therefore, please let your servant remain instead of the boy as a servant to my lord, and let the boy go back with his brothers. For how can I go back to my father if the boy is not with me? I fear to see the evil that would find my father."
> (Genesis 44:18, 30–34)

REVEALED

Joseph is dumbfounded by Judah's plea, and he sees exactly how much the hearts of his brothers have changed in 20 years. They are no longer scheming to sell him to slave traders—they are now making self-sacrificial pleas to be allowed to endure the punishment that belongs to another. Rather than deceiving his father, Jacob, Judah now feels compassion for him. His words, "For how can I go back to my father if the boy is not with me?" show that his biggest concern is not himself, but his father—he wants to spare his father agony and even death by heartbreak. Judah and his brothers have become men, worthy of carrying the mantle of leaders of the nation of Israel.

After Judah's speech, Joseph orders the room cleared of everyone except his brothers, and in the midst of loud tears, cries out, "'I am Joseph! Is my father still alive?'" (Genesis 45:3). The brothers' first reaction is shock and dismay, because they are afraid of what Joseph might do in retribution. He allays their fears immediately, though, telling them that their actions, though painful at the time, have turned out to be the means God used to preserve the nation of Israel:

> "I am your brother, Joseph, whom you sold into Egypt. And now do not be distressed or angry with yourselves because you sold me here, for God sent me before you to preserve life. For the famine has been in the land these two years, and there are yet five years in which there will be neither plowing nor harvest. And God sent me before you to preserve for you a remnant on earth, and to keep alive for you many survivors. So it was not you who sent me here, but God. He has made me a father to Pharaoh, and lord of all his house and ruler over all the land of Egypt." (Genesis 45:4–8, emphasis added)

In just a few words, Joseph shows his brothers the power of forgiveness. He is not harboring any anger or bitterness for their actions toward him—he is looking to the greater purpose behind the events of 22 years ago. If his brothers

Joseph reveals himself to his brothers. In the midst of their joyful reunion, Joseph tells them, "You must tell my father of all my honor in Egypt, and of all that you have seen. Hurry and bring my father down here." (Genesis 45:13)

had not sold him into slavery, he would not have risen to power in Egypt and had the foresight to prepare for the unspeakable famine now upon them. With no one to store grain for the lean years, Joseph and all his family would have perished, meaning that the entire Jewish race would have been wiped out. Joseph's sons and brothers became the heads of the 12 tribes of Israel, whose history makes up the unfolding story of God's redemption. God had promised to make a great nation of Abraham, Isaac, and Jacob, with descendants as numerous as the sand of the seashore and the stars of the sky. If Joseph had not been sent to Egypt 22 years ahead of time, God's promise would have failed and the nation of Israel would have been stillborn.

The brothers accept Joseph's freely offered forgiveness and spend time catching up and letting their bottled-up emotions flow freely. There is an abundance of weeping as they reconcile, but as joyful as his reunion with his brothers is, Joseph longs to see the face of his father, Jacob. He says to his brothers, "'Hurry and go up to my father and say to him, "Thus says your son Joseph, God has made me lord of all Egypt. Come down to me; do not tarry"'" (Genesis 45:9).

Joseph does not just want to see his father for old times' sake—he wants to help him and he knows he can provide for the family during the remaining years of the famine. He asks his brothers to convey this message to his father: "'You shall dwell in the land of Goshen, and you shall be near me, you and your children and your children's children, and your flocks, your herds, and all that you have. There I will provide for you, for there are yet five years of famine to come, so that you and your household, and all that you have, do not come to poverty'" (Genesis 45:10–11).

Pharaoh hears the news of Joseph's family and generously orders that Joseph send Egyptian wagons with the brothers so they will have room for their wives, children, and household goods. Joseph also sends money and clothes along with his brothers.

THE BROTHERS RETURN TO JACOB

The Qur'an records that when the brothers leave to return to Canaan, Jacob instinctively knows something important is happening regarding Joseph: "When the caravan departed their father said, 'I feel the breath of Joseph, though you will not believe me'" (Qur'an 12:94). Those who heard him indeed do not believe him, but as the brothers arrive home and say to Jacob, "'Joseph is still alive and he is ruler over all the land of Egypt,'" Jacob is awestruck. His heart "became numb, for he did not believe them" (Genesis 45:26). The Hebrew word used here actually means that Jacob's heart stops—he may be having some sort of seizure or physical episode.

The brothers explain what happened to Joseph and that he is now second in command over all the land of Egypt and wants the entire family to move there because of the famine. Jacob has a hard time believing them, but his reticence begins to turn to joy when he finally notices the presence of the distinctive Egyptian wagons that Joseph sent for him. His spirit revives and he says: "'It is enough; Joseph my son is still alive. I will go and see him before I die'" (Genesis 45:28). The Bible does not record any more of the conversation between Jacob and his sons. According to the Qur'an, the brothers ask forgiveness, saying: "'Father, implore forgiveness for our sins. We have indeed done wrong.'" Jacob replies: "'I shall implore my Lord to forgive you. He is forgiving and merciful'" (Qur'an 12:97–98). In any case, the outcome is favorable—the family is headed to Egypt, where Jacob will once again see his son.

A New Home

Once Jacob makes the decision to go to Egypt, 70 members of his household, including his sons and their families, gather their livestock and goods and load into Pharaoh's wagons for the journey. On the way, the entourage spends the night in Beersheba, a frequent place of worship for both Abraham and Isaac. Jacob offers sacrifices to the God of his fathers there, and that night, God visits him in a vision, assuring him that the decision to venture to Egypt is sound. "'I am God, the God of your father,'" he said. "'Do not be afraid to go down to Egypt, for there I will make you into a great nation. I myself will go down with you to Egypt, and I will also bring you up again, and Joseph's hand shall close your eyes'" (Genesis 46:3–4).

This promise means much to Jacob—God's previous promises regarding Jacob and his descendants had been connected with the Promised Land of Canaan. It is not easy for him to leave—the physical land has such a hold on Jacob that he later extracts a promise from his sons to bury him with his forefathers in Canaan. God's reiteration of his promise means that Jacob does not have to worry that he is somehow breaking the covenant; in fact, God specifically tells Jacob that his descendants will one day emerge from Egypt and return to the land he loves. The book of Exodus records the fulfillment of the promise, describing how the nation of Israel—grown to some 2 million souls from the original 70—marches out of the land of Egypt 430 years later to claim the Promised Land of Canaan. God's words to Jacob at Beersheba include

Getting the Numbers Right

In Acts 7:14, Stephen recounts the story of Joseph and says 75 members of Jacob's household went down to Egypt. The difference of 5 people (Genesis 46:27 says there were 70 settlers) is explained by the fact that as a Hellenist (a Jew who adopted Greek culture), Stephen used the Greek translation of the Old Testament known as the Septuagint, which includes in its count 5 people actually born in the land of Egypt: two sons of Manasseh, two sons of Ephraim, and one grandson of Ephraim.

The 70 counted people of Jacob's household who went to Egypt did not include servants. If their servants moved with them, the number actually settling in Egypt could have been around 3,000 people, based on other recorded numbers of servants in the Bible (Abraham roused 318 servants of his house in his attempt to rescue his nephew Lot in Genesis 14).

another promise as well—that his relationship with his son Joseph will be so close that Joseph will one day close Jacob's eyes after he dies.

Jacob and Joseph Reunited

With a renewed sense of purpose, Jacob dispatches Judah to lead the way to Goshen, located in the Egyptian Delta region, where Joseph has decided the family will settle. The geography of the area fits well with the needs of the herds and livestock that Jacob is bringing from Canaan. As his father comes near the end of his journey, Joseph cannot wait any longer—he rushes to Goshen, where he and Jacob share an emotional reunion. "He [Joseph] presented himself to him [Jacob] and fell on his neck and wept on his neck a good while. Israel said to Joseph, 'Now let me die, since I have seen your face and know that you are still alive'" (Genesis 46:29–30). Josephus says that "Jacob almost fainted away at this

Jacob and Joseph are reunited. Detail from a 13th century mosaic in a Florentine church.

unexpected and great joy; however, Joseph revived him, being yet not himself able to contain from being affected in the same manner, at the pleasure he now had; yet was he not wholly overcome with his passion, as his father was." Jacob is now looking face-to-face at the son he has not seen in more than 20 years. The sight is enough that he is satisfied and ready to die, although he will live for another 17 years.

Joseph is well aware of the proper Egyptian customs, so he brings five of his brothers before Pharaoh to obtain his blessing on their settlement in Goshen. Joseph knows that "every shepherd is an abomination to the Egyptians" (Genesis 46:34), so he wants to keep his family (who are all shepherds) separate from the Egyptians in the land of Goshen, both to protect their well-being and to preserve their identity as Israelites. Pharaoh asks the men what they do for a living, and they reply, "'Your servants are shepherds, as our fathers were'" (Genesis 47:3). They then ask permission to live in the land of Goshen: "'We have come to sojourn in the land, for there is no pasture for your servant's flocks, for the famine is severe in the land of Canaan. And now, please let your servants dwell in the land of Goshen'" (Genesis 47:4). Pharaoh responds to Joseph with a generous offer that shows his respect for Joseph:

> "Your father and your brothers have come to you. The land of Egypt is before you. Settle your father and your brothers in the best of the land. Let them settle in the land of Goshen and if you know any able men among them, put them in charge of my livestock." (Genesis 47:5–6)

Joseph then brings in his father, Jacob, to stand before Pharaoh, who inquires how old Jacob is. In typically pessimistic fashion, he answers: "'The days of the years of my sojourning are 130 years. Few and evil have been the days of the years of my life, and they have not attained to the days of the years of the life of my fathers in the days of their sojourning'" (Genesis 47:9). As full of conflict (much of it of his own making) as his life has been, however, it is now taking a turn for the better. He is set to enjoy a life full of the abundance of the best of the land of Egypt. Before he leaves Pharaoh's presence, he blesses Pharaoh, presumably in the name of his God (and not according to Pharaoh's god).

The official business transacted, Joseph provides food for his family in accord with the number of their dependents and settles them in "the best of the land, in the land of Rameses" (Genesis 47:11). Rameses was another name for the land of Goshen—a name that Moses, the author of Genesis, may have used to describe the area better. (In other places it is called Zoan or Tanis, after the cities of the region.) The region encompasses land along a branch of the Nile that has a reputation for being quite fertile. One ancient Egyptian writer described the productive land of Rameses this way, leaving no doubt that the Israelites truly were given the best of the land of Egypt:

> Its fields are full of good things, and life passes in constant plenty and abundance. Its canals are rich in fish; its meadows are green with vegetables; there is no end of the lentils; melons with a taste like honey grow in the irrigated fields. Its barns are full of wheat and durra, and reach as high as heaven. Onions and sesame are in the enclosures, and the apple-tree . . . blooms. The vine and the almond-tree and the fig-tree grow in its gardens. Sweet is their wine for the inhabitants of Keim. They mix it with honey.

11

FINAL RESTING PLACE

At this point, the narrative in Genesis skips ahead 17 years, during which "Israel settled in the land of Egypt, in the land of Goshen. And they gained possessions in it, and were fruitful and multiplied greatly" (Genesis 47:27). Jacob is now 147 years old and has had a front row seat to watch God's blessing unfold. As one scholar says, "For 17 years, Jacob was witness to the increase; he had a glimpse of God's promise to Abraham, Isaac, and himself in the process of being fulfilled." He has enjoyed watching his descendants, amazed at the turns his life has taken. Now, however, the time is drawing close for him to die. He wants to tidy up the last remaining details of his life, so he extracts a promise from Joseph that he will not bury him in Egypt, but will carry him to the tomb of his fathers in the Promised Land of Canaan.

Soon after this, as Jacob is even closer to death, Joseph takes his two sons,

Manasseh and Ephraim, to see their grandfather one last time. Jacob recounts for them the covenant God made with Abraham and repeated to him: "'Behold, I will make you fruitful and multiply you, and I will make of you a company of peoples and will give this land to your offspring after you for an everlasting possession'" (Genesis 48:4).

Jacob then uses the formal language of adoption to bequeath an inheritance to Joseph's two sons. "'Your two sons . . . are mine; Ephraim and Manasseh shall be mine as Reuben and Simeon are,'" he says (Genesis 48:5). In effect, Jacob is stripping the double portion of the inheritance reserved for Reuben, the firstborn son, and granting it to Joseph (possibly in gratitude for Joseph's generosity to his family) by way of his two sons. 1 Chronicles 5:1 explains why: "Reuben . . . was the firstborn, but because he defiled his father's couch, his birthright was given to the sons of Joseph the son of Israel, so that he could not be enrolled as the oldest son."

Jacob's decision means that Joseph's place as the head of a tribe of Israel is divided between his two sons. When the Israelites return to the land of Canaan more than 400 years later, they divide the land into 12 territories. The tribe of Levi receives no physical territory because they serve as priests to the nation and do not require land; Ephraim and Manasseh make up the difference, keeping the number of tribes at 12.

After Jacob announces Manasseh and Ephraim's inheritance, he wants to bless them by placing a hand on each of their heads. An old man, he has become blind and is confused about who the two boys are. His uncertainty brings to mind the confusion of Isaac, Jacob's father, as Jacob tricks him into bestowing Esau's firstborn blessing upon him. After Joseph explains that the boys are Jacob's grandsons, Jacob kisses them and says to Joseph, "'I never

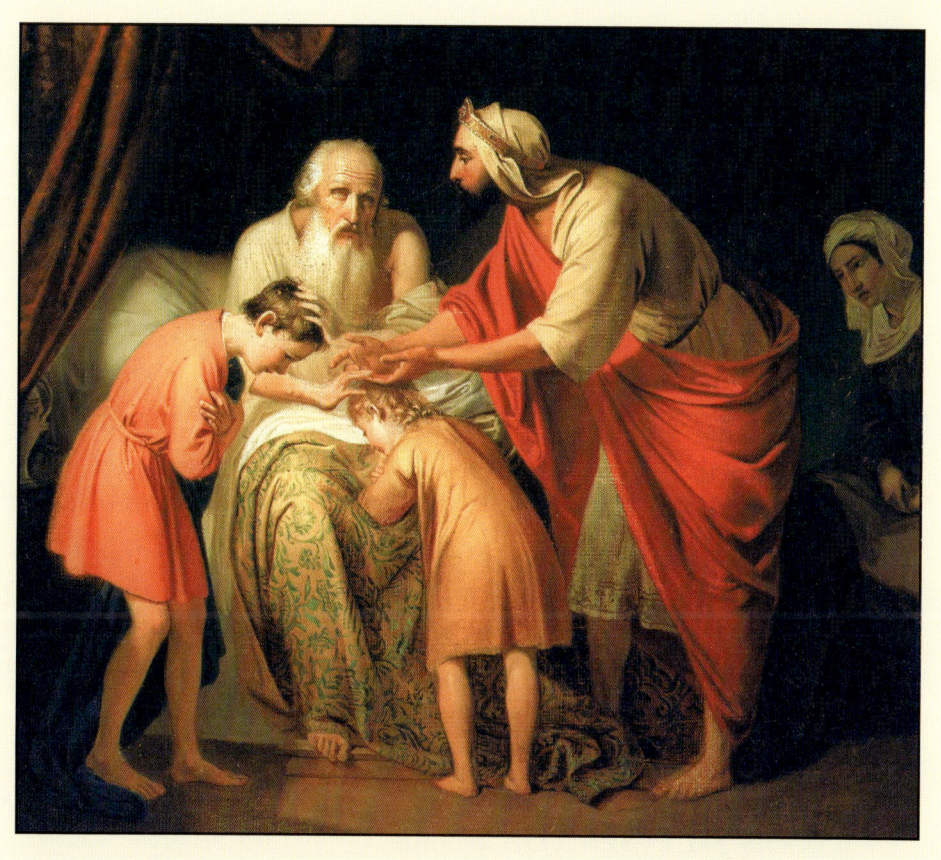

Jacob (seated) blesses his grandsons Ephraim and Manasseh. Joseph's attempt to uncross his father's hands is unsuccessful, so Ephraim receives the blessing that would normally go to the firstborn, Manasseh.

expected to see your face; and behold, God has let me see your offspring also'" (Genesis 48:11). Joseph presents his sons in the traditional manner to receive their blessing, with Manasseh (the firstborn) at Jacob's right hand, and Ephraim (the younger brother) at Jacob's left hand. Jacob, however, crosses his hands as he blesses the boys, asking God to carry his name through them and let them grow into a multitude on the earth.

Joseph then tries to move Jacob's hands to their correct positions, but Jacob refuses and tells Joseph that his younger son will become greater than the older—a prophecy that echoes Jacob and Esau's situation as well as Joseph's own ascent over his brothers. Jacob finishes the blessing with the words, "By you Israel will pronounce blessings, saying, 'God make you as Ephraim and as Manasseh'" (Genesis 48:20).

Scripture later records that Jacob's prophecy comes true—the tribe of Ephraim outnumbers the tribe of Manasseh, and Ephraim also outstrips his older brother in greatness—when the 10 northern tribes of Israel split from Judah and Benjamin after King Solomon dies, the name of the tribe of Ephraim becomes synonymous with the nation of Israel.

The author of the book of Hebrews in the New Testament also says that Jacob's blessing of the boys was an act of faith: "By faith Jacob, when dying, blessed each of the sons of Joseph, bowing in worship over the head of his staff" (Hebrews 11:21).

JACOB BLESSES HIS SONS

After he blesses Ephraim and Manasseh and immediately before he dies, Jacob gathers his sons to himself and issues a prophecy and blessing to each one. Judah and Joseph

> Jacob's last words to his grandsons in Genesis 48:20—"By you Israel will pronounce blessings, saying, 'God make you as Ephraim and as Manasseh'"—resound still today. Rabbi Telushkin says Jewish parents continue to use this phrase to bless their sons at the beginning of the Sabbath each week, and they bless their daughters with the phrase, "May God make you like Sarah, Rebecca, Rachel and Leah."

receive the longest and most bountiful blessings. Jacob prophesies about Judah—the brother who has become a leader—that "'the scepter shall not depart from Judah, nor the ruler's staff from between his feet'" (Genesis 49:10). Judah later becomes the largest tribe of Israel, and the line of Christ flows through his descendants.

The Qur'an also records that Jacob implores his sons to follow the faith of their fathers, saying: "'My children, God has chosen for you the true faith. Do not depart this life except as men who have submitted to him'" (Qur'an 2:132). He then asks them, "'What will you worship when I am gone?'" They reply, "'We will worship your God and the God of your forefathers Abraham and Ishmael and Isaac: the one God. To Him we will surrender ourselves'" (Qur'an 2:133).

After Jacob blesses his sons, he reiterates his desire to be buried with his fathers in Canaan. He gives specific directions, saying: "'I am to be gathered to my people; bury me with my fathers in the cave that is in the field of Ephron the Hittite, in the cave that is in the field at Machpelah, to the east of Mamre, in the land of Canaan, which Abraham bought with the field from Ephron the Hittite to possess as a burying place. There they buried Abraham and Sarah his wife. There they buried Isaac and Rebekah his wife, and there I buried Leah—the field and the cave that is in it were bought from the Hittites'" (Genesis 49:29–32). The covenant pull to be with his fathers, in the land that God has promised to them, stays with Jacob (Israel) until the very end. In Jacob's detailing of the specifics of the land, Robert Alter says, "Legal language is used to resume a great theme—that Abraham's offspring are legitimately bound to the land God promised them, and that the descent into Egypt is no more than a sojourn." And as another scholar says, "It was the last expression of Jacob's faith that all the promises which God had made regarding the land would yet come true." Then, after Jacob finishes directing his sons, he "breathed his last and was gathered to his people" (Genesis 49:33).

Jacob's Burial

When a patriarch in ancient societies died, time stood still. His people would gather to grieve for him and pay their respects—a process that could last for days. Such is the case with the death of Jacob. Immediately after Jacob breathes his last breath, Joseph falls on his father's face, weeping and kissing him, countless memories and affection spilling over.

Later, Joseph calls the physicians in Egypt to embalm his father. The embalming, or mummifying, process in Egypt (one of the first countries to introduce the practice) took about 40 days—the body had to be gutted, dried, and wrapped. According to Jewish legend, Joseph uses his riches and power to honor his father by ordering his body to be laid on a "couch of ivory, covered with gold, studded with gems, and hung with drapery of byssus and purple. Fragrant wine was poured out at its side, and aromatic spices burnt next to it."

After the embalming is complete, the Israelites and Egyptians continue mourning for another month, for a total of 70 days. Diodorus, an ancient writer, says 72 days was the customary period of mourning for a king. So great is the Egyptians' admiration for Jacob that they accord him almost the same privilege as one of their own kings.

When the time of mourning is over, Joseph asks Pharaoh to let him honor Jacob's last wish—that he be buried with his family in Canaan. It is a measure of Pharaoh's esteem for Joseph and for Jacob that he grants the request. The journey to Canaan includes all the ser-

Detail from a 13th-century French psalter, or book of psalms and prayers, showing Jacob's embalmed body being laid in the family tomb within the cave of Machpelah. By the time of Joseph, Egyptians had mastered the process of embalming, or mummification. It was important to Egyptians to preserve their bodies in as lifelike a manner as possible, for they believed that the body was the home for the soul and if the body were destroyed, the soul would have no resting place. As followers of God, Joseph and his family would not have believed this. Joseph knew Jacob's body would have to be well-preserved to endure the journey back to Canaan for burial, and he simply wanted to take the best care possible of his father, even in death.

This building in Hebron stands over the ancient cave tomb where Jacob is believed to have been buried, along with his grandparents Abraham and Sarah, and his parents, Isaac and Rebekah. Jacob's wife Leah is believed to have been buried there as well. Jews, Christians, and Muslims consider the Cave of the Patriarchs a holy site.

vants of Pharaoh, the elders of his household, and all the elders of the land of Egypt, as well as all the household of Joseph, his brothers, and his father's household. Only their children, their flocks, and their herds were left in the land of Goshen. And there went up with him both chariots and horsemen. It was a very great company. (Genesis 50:7–9)

This is a grand funeral procession, including everyone from high-ranking Egyptian officials to Hebrew shepherds. Jewish legend again tells of the luxuriant trappings that Joseph provided: "It [the bier on which Jacob's body rested] was fashioned of pure gold, the border thereof inlaid with onyx stones and bdellium, and the cover was gold woven work joined to the bier with threads that were held together with hooks of onyx stones and bdellium. Joseph placed a large golden crown upon the head of his father, and a golden scepter he put in his hand, arraying him like a living king."

The procession continues to a place called Atad in Canaan, where it halts for seven more days of "very great and grievous lamentation" (Genesis 50:10). The Canaanites see the magnitude of the Egyptians' grief over the death of Jacob and change the name of the threshing floor from Atad to Abel-Mizraim ("the mourning, or meadow, of Egypt"). Jacob's sons continue the journey and fulfill their promise to their father by burying him in the ancestral burying place alongside Abraham and Sarah, Isaac and Rebekah, and his own wife Leah. (The scriptures do not say when or how Leah dies, but she has been given the honor of burial in Jacob's family tomb.) Their task finished, Joseph, his brothers, and all who made the journey with them return to Egypt.

Jacob's sons live out the rest of their lives peacefully in Egypt, raising their families and watching over their flocks. Joseph's brothers have a moment of panic after Jacob dies, because they conclude with their father now gone, Joseph might finally take his opportunity for revenge. Instead, he tells them, "'Do not fear, for am I in the place of God? As for you, you meant evil against me, but God meant it for good, to bring it about that many people should be kept alive, as they are today'" (Genesis 50:19–20). One scholar says that Joseph's "wise, theological answer has gone down in history as the classic statement of God's sovereignty over the affairs of men."

Joseph lives to be 110. When the Israelites exit Egypt more than 400 years later, they carry his bones with them until they reach the Promised Land, where he is buried in the family tomb in the Cave of Machpelah. By then, the nation has been divided into 12 tribes named after Jacob's sons (except for Joseph—his sons Ephraim and Manasseh take his place). It is a fitting tribute to the last of the patriarchs.

Final Analysis

Jacob's is a twisted life made straight. Though struggle is a constant theme of his life, he survives his early troubles and learns to live according to the promises God has given him as the heir to his covenant. Despite the litany of troubles that arise within his family, it is still the family God uses to carry out his work. As one scholar puts it, "The divine plan for Jacob has been achieved, against human custom . . . and against human suitability."

Always a quiet man, "the chaos of his soul falls more into order," Blaikie says, as he learns to channel his persistence toward what God wants for him rather than what he wants for himself. And as he does so, God paradoxically blesses him in an earthly manner as well. He becomes wealthy beyond what most men dream of, with flocks and herds beyond counting.

Jacob's story is not just about him—it is about the people of God who descend from him, take his name as their name, and produce a lineage that leads straight through David to Christ. When Jacob is mentioned in the remaining pages of scripture, it is mostly in reference to the big picture of his life, rather than to his inconsistencies. In the end, he is a man who followed God, a man whom God used as the father of a nation. This is reflected in the many references to Abraham, Isaac, and Jacob (the three patriarchs) together in the Bible. The Psalms refer continuously to the God of Jacob, and the prophets speak often of the "house of Jacob" and of God redeeming Jacob and his people.

One does not have to wonder about Jacob's own assessment of his life. When he is blessing his grandsons just before he dies, he wraps the blessing in a summary of his own life. He has finally come to see the truth about the God with whom he has struggled for so long—this God had a purpose in mind for Jacob, and despite his best efforts to the contrary, God's "relentless grace," as Iain Duguid calls it, pursued him until he yielded. In spite of seasons of negativity and fear, Jacob clings to what he knows to be true, and he comes to know that the God of Abraham and Isaac has become his God as well. He says: "'The God before whom my fathers Abraham and Isaac walked, the God who has been my shepherd all my life long to this day, the angel who has redeemed me from all evil, bless the boys; and in them let my name be carried on, and the name of my fathers Abraham and Isaac; and let them grow into a multitude in the midst of the earth'" (Genesis 48:14–16).

It is a fitting conclusion to the life of Jacob. God has been his shepherd each day and has redeemed him from evil in order that his name could be carried on by multitudes of his descendants upon the earth. This, then, is Jacob, last of the patriarchs.

Notes

CHAPTER 1: WHY JACOB?

page 12: "was marked by conflict ..." Iain M. Duguid, *Living in the Grip of Relentless Grace: The Gospel in the Lives of Isaac and Jacob* (Phillipsburg, NJ: P & R Publishing, 2002), p. 64.

page 14: "It is a central tension ..." David Noel Freeman, ed., *The Anchor Bible Dictionary*, vol. 3 (Doubleday: New York, 1992), p. 602.

page 14: "is virtually unique ..." Robert Alter, *The Five Books of Moses: A Translation with Commentary* (New York: W. W. Norton, 2004), p. 265.

page 14: "scheming, conniving ..." Duguid, *Living in the Grip of Relentless Grace*, 27.

page 14: "he shows us the triumph ..." Duguid, *Living in the Grip of Relentless Grace*, 6.

page 14: "the archetypal picture ..." Duguid, *Living in the Grip of Relentless Grace*, 60.

CHAPTER 2: EARLY YEARS

page 18: "suffered torturous pain ..." Louis Ginzberg, *Legends of the Bible* (Philadelphia, Jerusalem: Jewish Publication Society, 1956), p. 149.

page 20: "abandoned himself to idolatry ..." Ginzberg, *Legends of the Bible*, 150.

page 20: "Jacob was a man perfect ..." quoted in James L. Kugel,

The Bible as It Was (Cambridge, MA, and London, England: Belknap Press of Harvard University Press, 1997), p. 200.

page 21: "Lordly, selfish, and stirring ..." William G. Blaikie, *Heroes of Israel: Abraham, Isaac, Jacob, Joseph and Moses* (Birmingham, AL: Solid Ground Christian Books, 2005), p. 190.

page 22: "Jacob proves quite wily ..." Rabbi Joseph Telushkin, *Biblical Literacy: The Most Important People, Events, and Ideas of the Hebrew Bible* (New York: William Morrow, 1997), p. 47.

page 23: "did not sell it ..." quoted in Kugel, *The Bible as It Was*, 208.

page 23: "the scorn [he] manifested ..." Ginzberg, *Legends of the Bible*, 153.

CHAPTER 3: DECEPTION

page 25: "morally problematic" Rabbi Joseph Telushkin, *Jewish Literacy: The Most Important Things to Know About the Jewish Religion, Its People, and Its History* (New York: William Morrow, 1991), p. 38.

page 29: "For each blessing . . ." Louis Ginzberg, *Legends of the Jews*, vol. 1. (Philadelphia: The Jewish Publication Society, 2003), p. 266.

page 29: "Isaac could not change ..." quoted in Kugel, *The Bible as It Was*, 210.

page 29: "I gave my blessing ..." Ginzberg, *Legends of the Bible*, 161.

page 31: "All the parties ..." Blaikie, *Heroes of Israel*, 195–96.

CHAPTER 4: DREAMS AND MARRIAGE

page 36: "was a singularly ..." Blaikie, *Heroes of Israel*, 207.

page 37: "looks for a speedy fulfillment ..." Blaikie, *Heroes of Israel*, 209.

page 38: "Jacob may have been ..." John MacArthur, *The MacArthur Study Bible* (Nashville, TN: Nelson Bibles, 2006), p. 56.

page 40: "to meet young maidens ..." Ginzberg, *Legends of the Bible*, 169.

page 40: "Their parallel nature ..." Duguid, *Living in the Grip of Relentless Grace*, 66.

page 41: "But Jacob was quite overcome ..." Flavius Josephus, *The Complete Works of Flavius Josephus* (Philadelphia: John E. Potter and Company, [1887?]), p. 46.

page 44: "both in drink ..." Josephus, *The Complete Works of Flavius Josephus*, 47.

page 44: "Laban carried out ..." quoted in Kugel, *The Bible as It Was*, 221.

page 44: "amid all Jacob's irritation ..." Blaikie, *Heroes of Israel*, 211.

page 45: "At Jewish weddings ..." Telushkin, *Jewish Literacy*, 33.

page 45: "O thou deceiver ..." Ginzberg, *Legends of the Bible*, 172.

page 45: "Is there a teacher ..." Ginzberg, *Legends of the Bible*, 172.

page 45: "There is an ironic fitness ..." Freeman, *The Anchor Bible Dictionary*, 603.

CHAPTER 5: BUILDING A FAMILY AND A FORTUNE

page 50: "unbecoming conduct ..." Ginzberg, *Legends of the Bible*, 175.

page 53: "My father is cunning ..." Ginzberg, *Legends of the Bible*, 170.

page 54: "the personification ..." Telushkin, *Biblical Literacy*, 58.

page 54: "Beware of sending him ..." Ginzberg, *Legends of the Bible*, 170.

page 54: "arch-villian . . . whose tongue ..." Ginzberg, *Legends of the Bible*, 177.

page 54: "a most uncomfortable master ..." Blaikie, *Heroes of Israel*, 212.

page 56: "sensory impressions ..." Alter, *The Five Books of Moses*, 164.

page 56: "The good man ..." quoted in Kugel, *The Bible as It Was*, 222.

CHAPTER 6: RETURN TO CANAAN

page 58: "He would cry to God ..." Ginzberg, *Legends of the Bible*, 184.

page 59: "a very elaborate procedure ..." Alter, *The Five Books of Moses*, 169.

page 61: "The tents are quickly struck ..." quoted in Blaikie, *Heroes of Israel*, 214.

page 63: "Rachel was a fitting wife ..." Duguid, *Living in the Grip of Relentless Grace*, 101.

page 64: "In exile ..." Freeman, *The Anchor Bible Dictionary*, 604.

CHAPTER 7: WRESTLING AND RECONCILIATION

page 69: "The night before the encounter ..." Telushkin, *Biblical Literacy*, 62.

page 71: "no name change ..." Telushkin, *Jewish Literacy*, 39.

page 71: "an amazing evaluation ..." MacArthur, *The MacArthur Study Bible*, 63.

page 72: "long, dark night ..." Duguid, *Living in the Grip of Relentless Grace*, 51.

page 73: "God 'filled the vacuum . . .'" Ginzberg, *Legends of the Jews*, p. 304.

page 77: "painted a picture ..." MacArthur, *The MacArthur Study Bible*, 65.

page 80: "a massacre of all males ..." MacArthur, *The MacArthur Study Bible*, 66.

page 80: "He could no longer live ..." Blaikie, *Heroes of Israel*, 231.

CHAPTER 8: RACHEL'S DEATH AND JOSEPH'S LIFE

page 82: "the sly loner ..." Freeman, *The Anchor Bible Dictionary*, 606.

page 85: "content to follow ..." Blaikie, *Heroes of Israel*, 236.

page 86: "It happened ..." Josephus, *The Complete Works of Flavius Josephus*, 50–51.

page 86: "Abraham and the other patriarchs ..." Freeman, *The Anchor Bible Dictionary*, 1077.

page 88: "beauty of his body ..." Josephus, *The Complete Works of Flavius Josephus*, 51.

page 88: "resembled his father ..." Ginzberg, *Legends of the Bible*, 194.

page 88: "It was not unnatural ..." Blaikie, *Heroes of Israel*, 237–38.

page 89: "affection of his [Joseph's] father ..." Josephus, *The Complete Works of Flavius Josephus*, 51.

page 90: "Jacob was pleased ..." Josephus, *The Complete Works of Flavius Josephus*, 51.

page 92: "Jacob recognized Joseph's coat . . ." Ginzberg, *Legends of the Jews*, p. 340.

CHAPTER 9: JOSEPH IN EGYPT

page 97: "The poor ate carrion ..." quoted in Blaikie, *Heroes of Israel*, 256.

page 97: "Nor did he open ..." Josephus, *The Complete Works of Flavius Josephus*, 56.

CHAPTER 10: A NEW HOME

page 112: "Jacob almost fainted away ..." Josephus, *The Complete Works of Flavius Josephus*, 61.

page 114: "Its fields are full ..." quoted in Blaikie, *Heroes of Israel*, 273

CHAPTER 11: FINAL RESTING PLACE

page 115: "For 17 years ..." MacArthur, *The MacArthur Study Bible*, 84.

page 118: "May God make you ..." Telushkin, *Biblical Literacy*, 90.

page 119: "Legal language is used ..." Alter, *The Five Books of Moses*, 290.

page 119: "It was the last expression ..." Blaikie, *Heroes of Israel*, 280.

page 120: "couch of ivory ..." Ginzberg, *Legends of the Bible*, 259.

page 122: "It [the bier on which ..." Ginzberg, *Legends of the Bible*, 261.

page 123: "wise, theological answer ..." MacArthur, *The MacArthur Study Bible*, 88.

page 124: "The divine plan for Jacob ..." Freeman, *The Anchor Bible Dictionary*, 607.

page 124: "the chaos of his soul ..." Blaikie, *Heroes of Israel*, 283.

page 125: "relentless grace ..." Duguid, *Living in the Grip of Relentless Grace*, 158.

Glossary

Apocrypha—in Greek, means "hidden things." A term signifying a collection of early Jewish writings excluded from the canon of the Hebrew scriptures. Jewish and Christian works resembling biblical books, but not included among the Apocrypha, are collected in the pseudepigrapha (including the testaments of Jacob's sons).

Bible—the term used since the fourth century CE to denote the Christian scriptures and later, by extension, those of various religious traditions. The Christian Bible includes the Old and New Testaments. The Hebrew Bible is just the Old Testament. See Hebrew scriptures below.

Canaan—an ancient region made up of Palestine or the part of it between the Jordan River and the Mediterranean Sea. It is the area of present-day Israel and the West Bank. In the Bible it is the Promised Land of the Israelites.

Haggadah—traditional Jewish literature, especially the nonlegal part of the Talmud.

Hebrew scriptures—the Torah, the Prophets, and the Writings, forming the covenant between God and the Jewish people that is the foundation and Bible of Judaism while constituting for Christians the Old Testament. Also called the Hebrew Bible.

Islam—world religion founded by the Prophet Muhammad. Founded in the seventh century CE, Islam is the youngest of the three monotheistic world religions (with Judaism and Christianity). An adherent to Islam is a Muslim.

Glossary

Jews—traditionally, descendants of Judah, the fourth son of Jacob, whose tribe, with that of his half brother Benjamin, made up the kingdom of Judah; historically, members of the worldwide community of adherents to Judaism.

Josephus—ca. 37–100 CE, Jewish historian and soldier. Josephus's historical works are among the most valuable sources for the study of early Judaism and early Christianity. He wrote The Jewish War; the famous Antiquities of the Jews, a history of the Jews from creation to the war with Rome; Against Apion, an exalted defense of the Jews; and his autobiography, or apologia.

Judaism—the religious beliefs, practices, and way of life of the Jews. The word Torah is employed when referring to the divinely revealed teachings of Jewish law and belief. Judaism is used more broadly, including also the totality of human interpretation and practice.

Midrash—any of a group of Jewish commentaries on the Hebrew scriptures compiled between 400 and 1200 CE and based on exegesis, parable, and haggadic legend. The Midrash provided rabbis with an opportunity to explain, expand, and fill in the gaps in the Torah.

patrilineal—relating to, based on, or tracing ancestral descent through the paternal line.

pharaoh—a king of ancient Egypt; a tyrant.

Philo—an Alexandrian Jewish philosopher known for his pioneering attempt to interpret the Hebrew scriptures in the terms of Neoplatonist philosophy.

Qur'an—the sacred text of Islam, considered by Muslims to contain the revelations of God to Muhammad.

Semitic—of or relating to the Semites or their languages or cultures. Also, of, relating to, or constituting a subgroup of the Afro-Asiatic language group that includes Arabic, Hebrew, Amharic, and Aramaic.

shekel—any of several ancient units of weight, especially a Hebrew unit equal to about a half ounce; a gold or silver coin equal in weight to one of these units, especially the chief silver coin of the ancient Hebrews.

Sheol—from the Hebrew language, the abode of the dead in the Bible.

Targum—a general name for a translation of the Hebrew Bible into Aramaic, a Semitic language related to Hebrew and spoken widely throughout the ancient Near East from the eighth century BCE onward. Some Targums contain frequent exegetical expansions of the biblical text.

Torah—the first five books of the Hebrew scriptures (Genesis, Exodus, Leviticus, Numbers, and Deuteronomy); a scroll of parchment containing the first five books of the Hebrew scriptures, used in a synagogue during services; the entire body of religious law and learning, including both sacred literature and oral tradition.

Further Reading

BOOKS FOR YOUNG READERS

Arthur, Kay, and Janna Arndt. *Extreme Adventures with God: Isaac, Esau, and Jacob*. Irvine, CA: Harvest House Publishers, 2005.

Davidson, Josephine. *The Old Testament: Ten Plays for Readers Theater*. Bellingham, WA: Right Book Company, 1992.

BOOKS FOR ADULTS

Blaikie, William G. *Heroes of Israel: Abraham, Isaac, Jacob, Joseph and Moses*. Birmingham, AL: Solid Ground Christian Books, 2005.

Duguid, Iain M. *Living in the Grip of Relentless Grace: The Gospel in the Lives of Isaac and Jacob*. Phillipsburg, NJ: P & R Publishing, 2002.

Ginzberg, Louis. *Legends of the Bible*. Philadelphia, Jerusalem: Jewish Publication Society, 1956.

Josephus, Flavius. *The Complete Works of Flavius Josephus*. Philadelphia: John E. Potter and Company, [1887?].

MacArthur, John. *The MacArthur Study Bible*. Nashville, TN: Nelson Bibles, 2006.

Telushkin, Rabbi Joseph. *Biblical Literacy: The Most Important People, Events, and Ideas of the Hebrew Bible*. New York: William Morrow, 1997.

———. *Jewish Literacy: The Most Important Things to Know About the Jewish Religion, Its People, and It's History*. New York: William Morrow, 1991.

Internet Resources

http://www.ancientegypt.co.uk/
  The British Museum's Web site dedicated to ancient Egypt. Good collection of information about ancient Egyptian life.

http://www.bartelby.com
  A good reference site that includes the Columbia Encyclopedia and the American Heritage Dictionary. Users can look up many references to Jacob and the Jews.

http://www.firstprescolumbia.org/Media/Audio/audio.asp
  A sermon series by Sinclair Ferguson on the life of Jacob. From 9.2.07 to 11.25.07.

http://www.imdb.com/title/tt0110175/
  A site describing the movie *Jacob*, based on his life.

http://www.jewishencyclopedia.com
  Contains the complete contents of the 12-volume *Jewish Encyclopedia*, originally published from 1901 to 1906. Includes information on Jacob.

http://www.myjewishlearning.com
>   Contains Jewish information and education for all ages and backgrounds. Provides well-written historical and scholarly information about Judaism, including multiple articles about Jacob.

http://www.sacred-texts.com
>   An enormous repository of electronic texts about religion, mythology, legends and folklore, and occult and esoteric topics. Texts related to Jacob include the Qur'an, the works of Josephus, *The Legends of the Jews* by Louis Ginzberg, and the pseudepigrapha, including the Testaments of Jacob's 12 sons.

http://www.si.edu/Engyclopedia_SI/nmnh/mummies.htm
>   A nice summary from the Smithsonian Institution about the Egyptian method of embalming, or mummification.

Index

Abraham
  character of, 13
  closeness to Jacob, 20
  death of, 16–17, 20
  God's covenant with, 6, 15–16, 23, 24, 33, 116
  and Isaac's birth, 16
  wealth of, 62
Acts passages, 111
Alter, Robert, 59, 119
Amos passages, 9
angels, 58, 70–71
Asenath (wife of Joseph), 95
Asher (Jacob's son), 49, 90–92, 99

Beersheba, 110
Benjamin (Jacob's son), 64, 83, 100, 101, 102, 104–106
Bethel, 35, 36, 51, *65*, 74, 80, 82, 83
Bethlehem, 83, 84–85
Bible, Jewish, 18
Bilhah, 48–49, 85
birthright, Jacob and Esau's trade of, 6, 19–23
Blaikie, William, 37, 80, 124
blessings
  after Jacob wrestles with angel, 70
  of Ephraim and Manasseh, 116–118
  Esau's plea for, 30
  God's presence with Joseph, 93
  God's promise for Jacob, 35–36, 103, 108
  Jacob's deception for, 12, 25–31
  and wealth, 7, 25

Canaan
  Abraham and Sarah's life in, 16
  Esau's wives from, 32
  famine in, 96
  God's promise for Israel, 11, 75, 111, 123
  Isaac and Rebekah's life in, 17, 24
  Jacob's return to, 57–67, 69–75, 86
Cave of Machpelah, 17, 50, 75, *84*, 85, 119, *121*, *122*, 123
children of Jacob, 12, 47, 49, 50
Christianity, 7–8, 14
1 Chronicles passages, 116
circumcision, 78
coat of many colors, 88, 89
currency, 20, 25, 86, 91

Dan (Jacob's son), 49, 90–92, 99
David, King, 51
deception
  about Joseph's disappearance, 31, 91, 92
  about Laban's stolen idols, 63
  for Esau's birthright, 6, 12, 13, 21–22
  for Isaac's blessing, 12, 25–31
  of Jacob, by Laban, 6, 13, 31, 45
  in Jacob's family, 13, 26
  of Shechem and Hamor, 78

Numbers in ***bold italics*** refer to captions.

Deuteronomy passages, 8
Dinah (Jacob's daughter), 50, 76–80
dreams, 35–36, 90, 94, **95**, 99
Duguid, Iain, 125

Edom, 18, 19, 22, 30, 85–86
Egypt
  famine in, 94, 95–103
  Jacob's life in, 110, 114, 115
  Joseph's life in, 93–114
  route to, *103*
El-bethel. *See* Bethel
El Shaddai, 33
embalming process, 120
Ephraim (Joseph's son), 95, 116–118
Esau
  birth of, 19, 22
  birthright trade, 12, 13, 21–22
  character of, 18, 19–23
  as father of Edom, 18
  hatred for Jacob, 31
  and Isaac's burial, 85
  loss of Isaac's blessing, 25–28
  marriages of, 32
  reunion with Jacob, 6, 66–68, 72–75
  sins of, 23
Exodus (book), 111

faith
  of Abraham, 16
  of Isaac, 17
  of Jacob, 34, 118, 125
  of Joseph, 94, 123
  and wealth, 7–9, 25
famine, 94, 96–103
favoritism
  God's absence of, 31
  of Isaac and Rebekah, 19–20, 26
  of Jacob toward Joseph, 87–89
  of Jacob toward Rachel, 42, 72

Gad (Jacob's son), 49, 90–92, 99
Galeed, 65
generosity
  of Joseph, 97
  of patriarchs, 8
  of Pharaoh, 109, 113, 120–122

Genesis passages
  Abraham's prosperity, 7
  Dinah's rape and aftermath, 76, 78–80
  God's control over childbearing, 48
  God's covenant with Abraham, 6, 15, 24, 33, 116
  Isaac and Rebekah's favoritism, 19
  Isaac prays for a child, 17
  Isaac's words to Esau after blessing Jacob, 30
  Jacob and Esau's parting, 86
  Jacob and Joseph, 88, 109, 110, 112
  Jacob and Laban's livestock agreement, 52
  Jacob blesses Ephraim and Manasseh, 116–117
  Jacob flees to Haran, 32
  Jacob grieves for Joseph, 92
  Jacob named Israel, 70
  Jacob obtains Esau's birthright, 22
  Jacob rebukes Laban, 64
  Jacob receives Esau's blessing, 27, 28
  Jacob returns to Bethel, 81, 82
  Jacob returns to Canaan, 57, 58–60, 67
  Jacob reunites with Esau, 66–68, 72, 86
  Jacob reunites with Joseph, 109, 110, 112
  Jacob's burial wishes, 119
  Jacob's dream at Bethel, 35–36, 82
  Jacob's life in Egypt, 110, 114, 115
  Jacob's love for Rachel, 41
  Jacob's negativity, 6, 101–102, 103
  Jacob's promise to God, 36, 82
  Jacob's prosperity, 6, 25, 56, 57, 73–74
  Jacob works for Laban, 6, 41, 52
  Jacob wrestles with angel, 69–71
  Joseph's birth, 50, 51
  Joseph's brothers ask for grain, 99–100, 102–103
  Joseph's brothers' guilt, 90, 105–106

Joseph's brothers plan to kill him, 90
Joseph's dream, 90, 99
Joseph's faith, 94
Joseph's preparation for famine, 97, 98–99
Joseph's reunion with brothers, 104, 106, 107, *108*, 109, 123
Judah, 102, 106, 119
Laban confronts Jacob about leaving, 62
Laban welcomes Jacob, 40
Leah's children, 47, 50
Pharaoh's generosity, 113
Rachel's children through Bilhah, 49
Rachel's desperation for a child, 47
Rachel steals Laban's idols, 63
Rebekah, 18, 32
Reuben's sin, 85
Goshen, 112, 113, 114

Hagar, *16*, 17
Haggadah. *See* legends, Jewish
Hamor, 76–78
Haran, 16, 34, 38–40
Hebrew Bible, 7–8
Hebrews passages, 23
Hebron, 50, 86, *87*
Hosea passages, 70
Hyksos, 100

idols, 60, 63, 81–82
Isaac (Jacob's father)
 birth of, 16
 blessing Jacob, 12, 25–31, 30
 burying Abraham, 16–17
 character of, 13
 children of, 17–19 (*See also* Esau; Jacob)
 death of, 85–86
 faith of, 17
 and God's covenant with Israel, 11, 24, 33
 and God's prophecy to Rebekah, 25–26
 marriage to Rebekah, 17
 wealth of, 6, 24–25

Isaiah passages, 9
Ishmael, 16–17
Islam, 14
Israel (name for Jacob), 14, 70, 71, 82
Israel (nation)
 division of, 8–9
 God's covenant with, 6, 11, 14, 15–16, 23, 24, 33, 116
 growth of, 111
 Jacob as father of, 18
 tribes of, 12, 79, 108, 116, 118, 124
Issachar (Jacob's son), 50, 90–92, 99
Issachar (Testament) passages, 44

Jacob, artistic images of
 blessing Ephraim and Manasseh, *117*
 burial, *121*
 confronting Laban, *43*
 deceiving Isaac, *13*, *29*
 dream at Bethel, *10*, *37*
 kissing Rachel, *41*
 with Laban, *53*
 mourning Rachel's death, *83*
 reconciliation with Esau, *73*
 return to Canaan, *59*
 reunion with Joseph, *112*
 struggle with angel, *70*
Jacob, characteristics of
 closeness to Abraham, 20
 continuing God's covenant with Israel, 11, 14, 18, 33, 111, 116, 124
 depression, 12, 13
 faith, 12, 13, 34, 118, 125
 favoritism, 42, 72, 87–89
 inheritance, 6, 25, 98
 love for Rachel, 40–42
 manipulation, 6, 12, 13, 22 (*See also* deception)
 negativity, 13, 101–102, 103, 113–114
 passivity, 12, 13, 79–80, 85
 patriarchal role, 18, 124
 prosperity, 12, 55–56, 57, 62, 73–74, 86, 98

quietness, 19, 21
renamed Israel, 14, 70, 71, 82
scholarship, 11–12, 20
transformation, 14, 64–65, 67, 124
understanding of birthright value, 22–23
Jacob, major events involving
  birth, 17–19
  blessing Ephraim and Manasseh, 116
  burial, 115, 119, 120–124
  burying Isaac, 85
  children, 12, 47, 49, 50
  death, 110, 112, 120
  deceiving Isaac for blessing, 12, 25–31
  dream at Bethel, 35–36, 51
  God's promises, 11, 35, 51, 111
  life in Haran, 38–56
  marriages, 12, 32, 33, 42
  murder of Canaanites, 78–79
  return to Canaan, 57–67, 69–75
  reunion with Esau, 6, 66–68, 69, 72–74
  reunion with Joseph, 109, 110–114
  trade for Esau's birthright, 6, 12, 13, 21–22
  working for Laban, 6, 13, 41–42, 51–52, 61–65
  wrestling with angel, 70–71
Jesus, teachings on wealth, 9
Job, 8
Joseph
  brothers' hatred toward, 89–92
  dreams of, 90
  faith of, 94, 123
  forgiveness of brothers, 123
  generosity of, 97
  interpretation of Pharaoh's dreams, 94, **95**
  Jacob's blessing for, 118–119
  Jacob's favoritism toward, 87–89
  marriage of, 95
  as Pharaoh's viceroy, 94–97
  as Potiphar's servant, 93
  in prison, 94
  reunion with family, 104–109, 112–114, 123
  seduction by Potiphar's wife, 93–94
  sold into slavery, 12, 90–92
Josephus, 86, 88, 89, 90, 97, 112–113
Judah (Jacob's son), 47, 90–92, 99, 102, 105–107, 118–119
Judaism, 14

Laban
  character of, 52–55, 57
  confrontation with Jacob, 61–64
  covenant with Jacob, 65
  Jacob's work for, 6, 51–52
  manipulation of Jacob, 6, 13, 42–45, 51–52, 55
  resentment of Jacob, 57
  search for stolen idols, **63**
  welcome for Jacob, 40
Leah (Jacob's wife)
  appearance of, 41
  burial of, 123
  children of, 47, **48**
  marriage to Jacob, 42, 46, 72
  rivalry with Rachel, 46–47, 49–50, 51
legends, Jewish
  angels' protection of Jacob, 58
  Esau's attempt to kill Jacob, 38
  Esau's sins, 23
  Jacob's burial, 120
  Jacob's favoritism toward Joseph, 88
  Jacob's journey to Haran, 38–40
  Jacob's love for Abraham, 20
  Jacob's rebuke of Leah, 45
  Jacob's return to Canaan, 45, 59
  Jacob's theft of Esau's blessing, 28
  Laban's exploitation of Jacob, 54
  on meeting young maidens, 40
  origin of, 18
  Rachel and Leah's mandrake trade, 50
Levi (Jacob's son), 47, 78–79, 90–92, 99, 116
lies. *See* deception
Luke passages, 7

MacArthur, John, 71
Machpelah. *See* Cave of Machpelah
Manasseh (Joseph's son), 95, 116–118
mandrakes, 49–50
marriages
  to Canaanite women, 32, 76–78
  of Esau, 32
  of Jacob, 12, 32, 33, 42
  of Joseph, 95
massebah, **65**
Matthew passages, 7, 9
Midrash, 18
money, 20, 25, 86, 91
mourning, 120

Naphtali (Jacob's son), 49, 90–92, 99

Peniel, 70
Pharaoh
  dreams of, 94, **95**
  generosity toward Joseph's family, 109, 113, 120–122
  promotion of Joseph, 94–95
polygamy, 43, 51
Potiphar, 93, 94
Promised Land, 11, 75, 111, 123. *See also* Canaan
prophecy to Rebekah, 18, 19, 21, 25–26
prosperity. *See* wealth
Proverbs passages, 8, 73

Qur'an
  descriptions of Jacob in, 14
  dietary restrictions in, 72
  Jacob asks God for forgiveness for sons, 110
  Jacob's dying instructions for his sons, 119
  Jacob's premonition about Joseph, 109
  Joseph's brothers plot his death, 89

Rachel (Jacob's wife)
  barrenness of, 47, 51
  beauty of, 41
  children of, 50–51, 64
  death of, 64, 83–84
  introduction to Jacob, 39–40
  Jacob's love for, 42, 72
  rivalry with Leah, 46–47, 49–50, 51
  theft of Laban's household gods, 60, 63
  tomb of, **84**
Rameses (Goshen), 112, 113, 114
Rebekah (Jacob's mother)
  character of, 20
  children of, 17, 18
  God's prophecy to, 18, 19, 21, 25–26
  marriage to Isaac, 17
  misery in later life, 32–33
  role in Jacob's deception of Isaac, 13, 25–26, 31–32
Reuben (Jacob's son), 47, 49, 84–85, 90–91, 90–92, 99, 100, 116
robe of many colors, 88, 89
Romans passages, 31

Sarah, 16
shearing, 59
Shechem, Jacob's life in, 74–80
Shechem (son of Hamor), 76–78
shekels, 91
Simeon (Jacob's son), 47, 78–79, 89, 90–92, 99, 101
sinews, dietary restrictions regarding, 71–72
standing stones, **65**

Talmud, 18, 72
Telushkin, Rabbi, 22, 25, 45, 69, 118
tithe, 36, 38
tribes of Israel, 12, 79, 108, 116, 118, 124

veils, 45

wealth
  and faith, 7–9, 25
  as God's blessing, 25
  of Isaac, 6, 24–25
  of Jacob, 6, 25, 98 (*See also* Jacob, characteristics of)
  measurement of, 20, 55, 86

Zebulon (Jacob's son), 50, 90–92, 99
Zilpah, 49

Illustration Credits

2: Erich Lessing/Art Resource, NY
10: Erich Lessing/Art Resource, NY
13: Erich Lessing/Art Resource, NY
16: ©2008 JupiterImages Corporation
21: Réunion des Musées Nationaux/Art Resource, NY
29: Erich Lessing/Art Resource, NY
30: Bildarchiv Preussischer Kulturbesitz/Art Resource, NY
37: Erich Lessing/Art Resource, NY
41: Erich Lessing/Art Resource, NY
43: National Gallery Collection/By kind permission of the Trustees of the National Gallery, London/Corbis
48: Elio Ciol/Corbis
49: ©2008 JupiterImages Corporation
53: Erich Lessing/Art Resource, NY
55: Used under license from Shutterstock, Inc.
59: Erich Lessing/Art Resource, NY
60: Erich Lessing/Art Resource, NY
63: The Art Archive/Palazzo dell'Arcivescovado Udine/Gianni Dagli Orti
65: istockphoto.com/Allan Schuler
70: Scala/Art Resource, NY
73: The Art Archive/Museo Tosio Martinengo Brescia/Aldredo Dagli Orti
77: Erich Lessing/Art Resource, NY
83: Arte & Immagini srl/Corbis
84: Library of Congress
87: Library of Congress
92: The Jewish Museum/Art Resource, NY
95: Erich Lessing/Art Resource, NY
96: © Dahesh Museum of Art, New York, USA/ The Bridgeman Art Library
103: © OTTN Publishing
105: The Jewish Museum/Art Resource, NY
108: © Musee des Beaux-Arts, Angers, France/Giraudon/The Bridgeman Art Library
112: Scala/Art Resource, NY
117: Alinari/Art Resource, NY
121: Erich Lessing/Art Resource, NY
122: Used under license from Shutterstock, Inc.

Cover photo: Bildarchiv Preussischer Kulturbesitz/Art Resource, NY

BENJAMIN T. HOAK is a freelance writer living in Owensboro, Kentucky, with his wife, Kelsey, and their sons, Carter and Taylor. He has also been a newspaper writer and a middle school teacher. He is a graduate of Kentucky Wesleyan College and is a fellow of the World Journalism Institute. His work has appeared in WJI's monograph series, *City* magazine, and the *Public Life Advocate*. He is also the coauthor of the forthcoming book *A Man as Priest in His Home*.